Praise for *Once Upon a Time in Shaolin*

"A bombshell new book." —New York *Daily News*

"An epic battle between colo⸺⸺⸺⸺⸺⸺⸺nd one of the blandest beta vill⸺⸺⸺⸺⸺⸺it down." —Patton ⸺⸺⸺⸺⸺⸺⸺ng ⸺⸺⸺ *Silver Screen Fiend*

"The rollicking narrative of the rap group Wu-Tang Clan's notorious efforts to create an album that, rather than being mass-marketed, would be valued like a work of art . . . But the book also invokes much deeper themes. It's about the group's efforts to rectify the fact that file sharing and streaming business models have rendered it nearly impossible for most musicians to make money from their work." —*strategy + business*

"Hold on tight . . . it's a roller coaster. . . . Money, art, danger, intrigue, glamour. It's all here, and with Bozorgmehr by our side, we know we are going to experience it all. . . . [A] breakneck dive into a world we never thought we'd be privy to." —*PopMatters*

"[An] utterly candid work . . . Bozorgmehr's stirring account gives readers the insider's view of musical outlaws who possessed the best intentions of elevating hip-hop from its street moorings to more stylish, chic surroundings, and whose efforts exploded in a crisis of bad media coverage and soulless pharmaceutical drug merchants." —*Publishers Weekly*

"[Bozorgmehr's] insider's knowledge of the process drives this fascinating story, full of suspense and surprises. A detailed, compelling look at of one of the music business's most interesting stories." —*Booklist*

"A fantastic, gripping read from start to finish, *Once Upon a Time in Shaolin* takes us to the heart of the action and shows us what really went on behind closed doors with Wu-Tang's most controversial album. A must-read for hip-hop fans and for anyone who wants the inside story into one of music's most talked-about events." —Paul Edwards, author of *The Concise Guide to Hip-Hop Music*, *How to Rap*, and *How to Rap 2*

"*Once Upon a Time in Shaolin* offers a front-row seat as Wu-Tang Clan's maverick, idealistic attempt at a statement on the current state of the music industry and the symbiosis of art and money backfires, turning into a surreal caper featuring monumental ambitions, even more monumental egos, Bill Murray, the FBI, replica AK-47s, and, yes, arguably the most hated man in America. It's a music book unlike any other." —Paul Fischer, author of *A Kim Jong-Il Production*

ONCE UPON A TIME IN SHAOLIN

ALSO BY CYRUS BOZORGMEHR

THE SYNDICATE

THE UNTOLD STORY
OF WU-TANG CLAN'S
MILLION-DOLLAR
SECRET ALBUM, THE
DEVALUATION OF MUSIC,
AND AMERICA'S NEW
PUBLIC ENEMY NO. 1

CYRUS BOZORGMEHR

ONCE UPON A TIME IN SHAOLIN

FLATIRON
BOOKS
NEW YORK

ONCE UPON A TIME IN SHAOLIN. Copyright © 2017 by Cyrus Bozorgmehr. All rights reserved. Printed in the United States of America. For information, address Flatiron Books, 120 Broadway, New York, NY 10271.

www.flatironbooks.com

Designed by Jonathan Bennett

The Library of Congress has cataloged the hardcover edition as follows:

Names: Bozorgmehr, Cyrus, author.
Title: One upon a time in Shaolin : the untold story of Wu-Tang Clan's million dollar
    secret album, the devaluation of music, and America's new public enemy no. 1 /
    Cyrus Bozorgmehr.
Description: First edition. | New York : Flatiron Books, 2017.
Identifiers: LCCN 2017005470| ISBN 978-1-250-12527-9 (hardcover) |
    ISBN 978-1-250-12528-6 (ebook)
Subjects: LCSH: Wu-Tang Clan (Musical group). One upon a time in Shaolin. |
    Sound recording industry—Moral and ethical aspects. | Shkreli, Martin.
Classification: LCC ML421.W8 B69 2017 | DDC 782.421649092/2—dc23
LC record available at https://lccn.loc.gov/2017005470

ISBN 978-1-250-17783-4 (trade paperback)

Our books may be purchased in bulk for promotional, educational, or business use. Please contact your local bookseller or the Macmillan Corporate and Premium Sales Department at 1-800-221-7945, extension 5442, or by email at MacmillanSpecialMarkets @macmillan.com.

First Flatiron Books Paperback Edition: 2022

10 9 8 7 6 5 4 3 2 1

CONTENTS

ONCE UPON A TIME IN SHAOLIN

PROLOGUE

2007

"Have you ever heard of the Wu-Tang Clan?"

Well, of course I had. Didn't explain what the fuck this rather placid-looking Moroccan chap in glasses had to do with them though. Maybe he ran the local fan chapter.

"That's my crew—I'm part of the extended Clan. Name's Tarik."

This dude's going to try and sell me a villa next. It was just too ludicrous to contemplate. I smiled and nodded indulgently.

But there was something about the way he'd dropped it. No big thing—didn't oversell it, no preening or fluffing of feathers. He was either one seriously left-field motherfucker or a gloriously incompetent bullshit artist. Only time and a Google search would tell. And yet, as the conversation took its flow, something sparked under an African sky.

We had been introduced at a lunch party hosted by the sculptor and author Jimmy Boyle on a crystal-clear day in Marrakech. Despite my suspicions that Tarik might be insane or at least a dangerous fantasist, we were rolling deep within minutes. By sundown, we had set the music world to rights and he still hadn't had a sip from the vine, while I was about three bottles to the good. A set of supremely ephemeral breakthroughs on a warm spring breeze.

And then what seemed like the most absurd of all the ideas floated.

"I've been thinking about a single copy of an album, sold privately," said my new friend.

"Sounds dangerously elitist," I replied . . . even if you could argue that it was an evolutionary adaptation generated by the economic meltdown within music.

The much-heralded democratization of the digital had, like so many revolutions before it, morphed into a new tyranny. Recorded music was increasingly viewed as worthless, and getting heard was more difficult than ever as the ease of production and digital distribution created a new enemy—saturation. Independents were buckling, development budgets were a distant memory, and perhaps most worrying of all, the perception of music had shifted into something between voracious consumerism and a God-given right.

But commodifying music even further and placing it squarely in the hands of the wealthy? That was a step too far for me.

We said our goodbyes without any exchange of numbers or gushing promises—but it had been an intriguing conversation. Still needed to do that Google search, though.

And there it was . . . Wu-Tang-affiliated producer and rapper Cilvaringz. Well, fuck me . . .

2009

There's nowhere on this earth quite like Marrakech. Cast from the sands of a thousand years, her pockmarked battlements sigh cheerfully through the ravages of time. Labyrinths burrow into shadows of still reflection, pause for a quick cup of tea, and then dance the rhythms of lusty commerce. Tucked behind the veil, shady courtyards envelop themselves in the sweet scent of orange blossom, while out in the thoroughfares, an indulgent chaos reigns by popular acclaim. And away in the distance, the cloud-capped majesty of the Atlas Mountains nods sagely through the ages as horns blast, motorbikes chug in dissonant song, and tribal drums ring out the chant.

Marrakech's reputation for bohemianism is both thoroughly merited and eloquently contrived—much like bohemianism anywhere. Naturally there was a sense of privilege to anything quite so theatrically self-aware, but the first wave of flamboyant creatives who forged its reputation were gorgeously genuine. Crushed velvet capes and eccentric old aristocrats, barking mad painters and tragic diplomats tripped the oriental fantastic, and before you knew it, Marrakech was a byword for cosmopolitan style, a caravanserai for the international aesthete.

I had been here on and off now for three years. I traveled extensively for projects of all stripes and saw Marrakech as something of a refuge from my own mischief. I behaved here, nurturing a normal existence rather than staying awake for days on the jagged edge of pressure like I invariably did on a mission. While reveling in the town's joyous innocence, I clung to the contemplative life, preferring to wake at dawn to get some work done in a cloistered silence, but as a result, I had acquired hermit status in the social calendar. My long-suffering wife was less than impressed, especially when photos of me clearly having the time of my life kept popping up to document the jobs I'd been on, so when she suggested we engage in some vaguely meaningful way with Marrakech's impending art biennale, I felt I was a "fuck that" away from divorce.

The Marrakech Biennale's remit seemed to be assembling a mix of local and international art in a series of locations around the city, from crumbling palaces to exclusive boutique hotels. The opening cocktail party offered little hope for a visceral cultural experience; it felt like someone had satirized an artsy circle jerk in Chelsea, transplanted it to a palm-strewn rooftop, and used the local populace as an abstract string to a bullshit bow. But that wasn't a fair impression of the event as a whole, and as the days unfolded, we attended a range of exhibitions, installations, and talks, many of which were undoubtedly positive for the city's cultural life. There was perhaps more talk than evidence of cross-cultural engagement, and despite there being Moroccan art for Western collectors and Western art for Moroccan collectors, it did at times feel that there was largely fuck-all for the average Moroccan bar a couple of headline street pieces. It was one of those things that started off with the best of intentions but accidentally ended up elitist because it just couldn't stem its own tide.

Having been to a series of talks by Moroccan authors and filmmakers, I found myself trudging toward the Bahia Palace, one of the major exhibition centers, with my good mate Nick, and as we approached the entrance, who should we bump into? Yep—you guessed it. Cilvaringz and his wife, Clare.

We were delighted to see one another despite having made absolutely no effort in the intervening three years to get together for a drink or something, like normal people would. But the kind of connections that feel totally natural after three years and one intense conversation are far more valuable than vats of synthetic small talk, and I knew instantly that whether the art was transcendental or reminiscent of a 1970s novelty store, we were going to have some fun.

Cilvaringz was on the board of the Biennale, and as we strolled around the palace, he grew increasingly frustrated at the kind of money that had gone into the more forgettable exhibits. From buckets to paper planes to a couple of old bed frames, it threw up an instant mirror to the increasingly tortured state of music.

Grabbing a coffee afterward, we settled in for a postmortem. It wasn't that we were buying into the inverted snobbery of needing art to be figurative or the old "my six-year-old could do better" chestnut. Testing boundaries and the kaleidoscope of perception was what contemporary art was all about—be it a monochrome canvas or a pile of industrial rubble. But the line between high concept and complete bollocks was fraying, and this wasn't saying anything new. It was just really, really—mediocre.

And while buckets were selling for five figures, an ever-diminishing pool of people was prepared to pay for music. For albums that take years to make and have every ounce of a musician's heart and soul in them.

What was it that gave someone the barefaced balls to sell paper planes for thousands, while a new song gets ninety-nine cents at best and more likely gets torn out of the torrentsphere?

The ninety-nine-cent price tag was about volume, of course. The music industry model was always based on two main foundations—mass production and egalitarianism. An artist sells one original piece, or limited-edition prints, but a musician can sell millions of units. All of them are affordable, and outside of rare editions, everyone has a shot at buying them with no one paying more or less than anyone else.

But that was the architecture of the predigital world. A world in which people would grow increasingly excited as an album release date approached; where they rushed down to the record store and queued alongside others they shared a community with. And then glided home on a high, lovingly unwrapped their album, read the sleeve notes, listened for months, soundtracked highs and lows, vibrant peaks and calamitous troughs, and then mounted it on a shelf as an expression of identity. In other words, they treated it like art.

There was a pilgrimage to the acquisition of new music—even if it was two blocks away at Tower Records. And the emotional and financial investment people poured into music was relative to their experience of it, at least in some way. Tragically, in a weird evolutionary flaw, the less effort people have to make for something, the less they value it. And while that investment doesn't have to be economic—if you run twenty miles for an album, or do a hundred push-ups for a single, that's still you infusing an end product with a sacrifice. In the modern age, that sacrifice is almost always represented by money, so does placing economic value on something directly affect how we experience it? That's a very uncomfortable question.

Cilvaringz was getting increasingly animated. The table was taking the brunt of it. "People don't see music as art anymore. They don't see it as something valuable. That has to change, and right now—I might just be working on a project with RZA that I hope will start a real debate."

I really liked this guy. Fucking switched on, and a great energy. I looked forward to our next meeting. Still didn't swap numbers, though.

2013

Tranquillity shattered as the phone yelped into life. Fumbling around blindly, I smacked it into the bedside table a couple of times for good measure and peered through the mists at the name. Mr. S . . . Well, who else would be calling me at 3 a.m.? By this time tomorrow I'd either be halfway to the Arctic Circle, taking a crash course in cryptocurrency, hiring a team of archaeologists, or something similarly fucking random. This was as close to a Batphone ringing as I got—if Mr. S was calling me, then some kind of drama was imminent.

My qualifications are, shall we say, abstract. My role in so many of the creative projects I'd been involved with over the years had been subsidized by my work as a consultant to some of Mr. S's more unconventional investments. Doing a spot of consultancy for the bizarre on the side had been a real blessing in allowing me to follow my heart through sound systems, warehouse raves across Europe, giant immersive experiences, and passion projects in their infancy. Much as I fancied myself as a Mr. Wolf for the nonhomicidal, the reality was far more mundane—if it was fucking ridiculous and no one else on Mr. S's rather conservative team would touch it, I'd get a call. We had an understanding, though—an unspoken respect based on raw instinct.

"Cyrus," he said, with something vaguely approaching cheeriness. Sort of like a kindly but extremely demanding uncle.

"Morning, boss—hope you and the family are well."

"Tip-top," he replied, in that curiously anachronistic vernacular that always made me crack a smile.

He briefed me on a groundbreaking musical project he'd funded and asked if I would be willing to act as an advisor. He didn't fuck around, so if it had piqued both his interest and his checkbook it was almost certainly going to be an intriguing mission. There were two people I'd be directly liaising with if they approved my place on the board—a Mr. Robert Diggs and a Mr. Tarik Azzougarh, neither of whom I'd ever heard of.

And then he casually mentioned the Wu-Tang Clan and everything sharpened into vivid focus. It couldn't be . . . but then how many Tariks could there possibly be in the Wu-Tang ecosystem?

Robert Diggs, though. Who the fuck was that? Information was but a quantum second away, and suddenly there it was. The RZA.

"Roger that," I replied. Ten-four.

QUEST

I needed to know who and what I was dealing with. Grabbing the Internet by the scruff of the neck, I pored over Wu-Tang history, interviews, music, and lyrics until I had a relatively solid picture of Clan dynamics and a feel for RZA, the de facto leader and producer. I was fascinated by the Clan's interplay as a whole, from explosive positivity to edgy discord, but knowing that I would be working primarily with Cilvaringz and RZA, I needed to get a handle on what kind of people they might be and how their histories would inform where we went from here.

The story of the Wu-Tang Clan has been extensively documented elsewhere, and I won't retell it in these pages. But the question of how Cilvaringz ended up producing this record and indeed how the fuck he had managed to make it from provincial Holland to Shaolin is one that needs resolving.

It was quite the tale. Somewhere between a mythological quest and a remix of the American dream.

It all began in archetypal style . . . on a basketball court. It was 1993 and the concrete was running hot with hip-hop fire. Jostling for the freshest cuts to throw down while playing, Tarik

"Cilvaringz" Azzougarh and his friends were sending up the jumps on a freestyle spin as they brought the latest beats court-side. On a sunny morning in Tilburg, Netherlands, one of his pals swaggered onto the court juggling a cassette tape in his hands, and by the toothy grin on his face, he either had some seriously dope beats on the chrome or some cutting-edge audio porn. Turned out it was neither. He was brandishing his demo.

Cilvaringz and the others rocked back in respect. This mother-fucker had just flicked the switch from passive to active. He had dared to take that first step, and in doing so, cracked open all of their imaginations. The hunt was on for some instrumentals to lay down on, a microphone and a tape deck to record with as the inspiration started to flow. It was a real team effort, too, no battles or bullshit ego competition, just a group of friends bouncing vibes and ideas, swapping beats and pushing each other further, every last man whooping up his brother's rhymes.

Dre had dropped *The Chronic,* Snoop was rolling out the G Funk flavors, but for Cilvaringz, the pantheon was dominated by a phalanx of ruckus-inciting, neck-protecting, sword-swinging, chess-playing, temple-dwelling, badass motherfuckers called the Wu-Tang Clan. There wasn't all that much you could do to rep the movement in the heartland of Holland except be-come the most dedicated fan you could be, and Cilvaringz set about the mission with steely aplomb, all the while tightening up the tides on the mic.

In 1997, just as Cilvaringz and his friends were preparing a trip to New York, a thought slid into his consciousness and be-gan to take root. Before long, that initial thought had hoisted a flag, got some supplies in, and pretty much annexed his entire focus. Would the Clan take him on? Maybe not at parity, but on a label, as an affiliate—part of the Wu family. The prospect was almost too tantalizing to bear.

He instantly banished the idea as ridiculous, a pipe dream with some angel dust stuffed into the bowl—there was no fucking way. But ridiculous was a far cry from impossible, and his stubborn determination, quick-fire intellect, and unbridled passion all hunkered down into a team huddle for a motivational talk from the id. The superego was benched, the id got a line on some steroids, and the die was cast. If Shaolin disciples could make pilgrimages to the eternal heights of Song Mountain in China to fall prostrate in the Hall of Heavenly Kings, then he could damn well track down the Hall of Heavenly Beats somewhere in the tristate area.

With optimism and self-belief flooding through his veins, Cilvaringz stepped off at JFK and rode the arteries into the city's beating heart. Possibility ricocheted through his synapses as he rounded Forty-second Street and stepped into the Times Square arena . . . where suddenly, the music died. The needle came flying off the string-heavy soundtrack and the epic build tumbled into the abyss. He was surrounded by the neon shadows of his dream.

The Wu were huge. In '97, they were Grammy nominated; they'd smashed the living fuck out of every album they'd done; they'd redefined fashions, record deals, slang, and music in a searing flash of uncontrollable energy. Four years after their first album, *Enter the Wu-Tang (36 Chambers),* had set the charges, they were one of the biggest groups in the world. But it was one thing to know that intellectually, entirely another to see it mounted in glorious Technicolor.

Times Square was awash with the Wu. The new album,

Wu-Tang Forever, was getting ready to strike, and everywhere Cilvaringz looked, there were twenty-foot banners and digital screens seeming almost to mock his enthusiasm. Everywhere he went that trip, the W followed him, but not in a "signs to your destiny" kind of way—no, it was more of a "get your dreams in check" whiplash to the heart. Billboards, newsstands, Virgin Megastore displays, you name it, the Wu were ruling it, and with every new W, the dream faded further into the never.

Show me a decent myth or a solid American dream and I'll show you the second-act moment of despair. That plunge into the cauldron of overwhelming odds when our hero is beaten into submission and he is a blade's width from surrender. Just don't ever forget the third act.

Limping back to Holland carrying a suitcase stuffed with clothes and vinyl, Cilvaringz was dusting his self-belief off within minutes of being back on the court. Basketball kept things on a meditative track, and the dream began to rise slowly back from the ashes. The Clan had announced an Amsterdam show in May, and as he snapped up his ticket, he wondered if he might find fresh inspiration amid the strobes.

Dedication didn't come comfy, and as the day of the Amsterdam gig dawned, Cilvaringz and his crew were in line braving the cruel joke of the Dutch summer as the wind howled and the rains slammed down from the sky. Piling into the venue when the doors opened, they steamed down the middle of the hall, pushing as close to the front as they possibly could. It was an epic show—three hours of high-octane mayhem, and even then, the Clan weren't done. The legacy they'd leave wouldn't be through performance alone . . . Inspiration. Generation. Foundation.

With the crowd going nuts and a deafening roar for the encore, the Clan announced a freestyle session for local talent. Surely this was Cilvaringz's moment. He froze. This was some serious deep-end shit—a million miles from a studio audition. This was a sweat-soaked roller coaster through a packed hall of thousands yelling their throats dry. His body seized up—trapped in slow motion, before fate and family both took a hand.

His cousin stuck a knee square into his back and gave Cilvaringz an almighty shove toward the stage. Elbows flew in disgust as this kid came bulldozing through. Every last guy there fancied himself a rapper, so the second the freestyle was announced, the crush was on. But his cousin kept the pedal to the metal and forced Cilvaringz through the cracks until the lip of the stage was within touching distance. Glancing down, Method Man and Ol' Dirty Bastard clocked this kid seemingly smacking all comers out of the way, as the stumble from his cousin's push was mistaken for kick-ass confidence. Well, THAT motherfucker looked like he meant business. And he looked kinda comical, too. They hauled him up onstage without a second's hesitation, and there he was . . . onstage with the Wu-Tang Clan and a microphone thrust into his hand. No time to think, no time to question, no time to process. Silence . . . a spinback . . . and GO.

It was a flow best described as panicked, but it had potential. The crowd went with it, which was the first battle won, and as he shot glances to either side, Method Man and Ol' Dirty continued to flank him, feeling the vibes and backing his play. As if by alchemy, the terror had dissolved into a euphoric skydive. Confident enough to move from the spot he'd been rooted to since being elevated, he got his kinetic on and looked around to see how the Clan were reacting. RZA was surveying things from a strategic position by the decks, and Cilvaringz noticed a wink and an interested look shoot back between RZA and Ol' Dirty. Dirty was loving it—this was some real community outreach shit.

Cilvaringz didn't find out until years later, but the knowing smiles between the Clan had less to do with his magnetic rap talent than the sheer comedic spectacle of what they were witnessing. Here was this total nerd in glasses, a retro haircut that even the seventies didn't want back, clad head to toe in baggy hip-hop threads and rapping his heart out. It was hilarious. Not in a mocking way—in a really warm way. RZA immediately drew a parallel to Clark Kent: all spectacles and buttoned-down exterior, but give the boy a mic and see the lion roar.

He finished to a cheering crowd, and as he drank in a round of hearty backslaps from all the members, RZA pulled him aside. "Listen, kid . . ."

It was short but oh, so sweet. RZA had liked what he'd seen. He was in the process of starting an international Wu roster of new artists, and off the back of that performance, he wanted Cilvaringz involved.

A golden glow of triumph, redemption, and destiny washed across Cilvaringz. This was it. He'd done it. Victory was his. This was his break, his life-changing moment. And then, before he could seal the deal with some contact information, the stage erupted in a gigantic clusterfuck.

Ol' Dirty Bastard was the architect of both Cilvaringz's lightning ascendancy and his equally dazzling fall from grace. He was a red-blooded international megastar, and having switched his gaze from the kid onstage to a luxuriously inviting pair of breasts, he began wrapping his hands round the magnificent orbs bouncing before him. The young lady took the compliment in the spirit it was intended, but her boyfriend didn't see matters in quite the same freewheeling way. Wu or no Wu—get your fucking paws off my girl, motherfucker. A punch was thrown, a crew materialized behind the spurned lover, and before Cilvaringz could say "Yes Please," a massive fight careered across the stage and security guards started dropping from the rafters. The Clan were bundled offstage while all nonmembers, including the newly minted Wu affiliate, were tossed ignominiously back into the melee below.

So close . . . so fucking close. The words "Fuck yeah" frozen on his lips. Frozen forever, it seemed.

Well, at least he had some bragging rights to show for it, and like any other sane individual, he milked the story to fuck. He could dine out on that for years, but while it would always remain a great story, it was consigned to the "also-rans" of the nearly department. Weeks passed, and as a comedown set in, his restless mind was dominated by what might have been. There was only one thing for it. He'd go find RZA.

So where do you start looking for the Abbot of the Wu-Tang Clan? Well, he narrowed things down to New York, trimming the size of the haystack to a mere ten million people, and as soon as he could, he booked a flight to Gotham. And then another. And another five after that.

Penniless and operating out of the Vanderbilt YMCA, Cilvaringz began pinpointing strategic sites on the battlefield. And the first fortress he turned his sights on was Wu Wear in Staten Island, the apparel store for the discerning badass. It was a long shot at best; the chances of anyone integral to the group hanging out by the fitting rooms were slim, but it was a start. A rather disappointing start, as it turned out. Met by an avalanche of blank stares and eventually a security guard, Cilvaringz beat a tactical retreat back out to the sidewalk. And as he raised his eyes and glanced across the road, another W appeared like a vision of the angels. And what was this Shangri-la of salvation? It was Wu Nails. Yep, you heard. The Wu-Tang nail salon.

The mere fact that there was a nail salon out there rocking the W did rather emphasize just how big the Clan had become. This was the same period where the name was so all-encompassing that RZA had been approached by developers to open a Wu-Tang theme park in Florida. It might be a nail salon, but it was a Wu nail salon and that was a fucking start, so Cilvaringz crossed the road to do some professional loitering. It was always going to be slightly awkward, what with him not really looking like he was in the market for a manicure, so he just kind of embedded himself outside on hope's paving stone. The ladies inside were mystified. I mean, they'd met their fair share of weirdos, but this was right up there. Did they have a pervert on their hands or what?

He screwed his courage to the sticking point, pulled himself together, and strode in. There were sharp intakes of breath and some kissing of teeth, and three of the manicurists blocked his way. "Can we help you?" they inquired skeptically.

Cilvaringz launched into his story, describing the events in Holland and laying his cards on the table. He had a package that he needed to get to RZA somehow—his demos, his lyrics, and a series of heartfelt letters, pitched to actually arrest RZA's attention and not just gush like a superfan. As he finished his tale of woe and suicidal optimism, two ladies emerged from the shadows trying desperately to stifle a giggle.

It was RZA's mother and sister. And their faces radiated sym-

pathy. They took the package off Cilvaringz's hands and promised they'd get it to Bobby (RZA's real name). They wished him
luck, honored his persistence, and sent him on his way with a
spring in his step and their phone numbers in his pocket.

RZA's sister Sophia was incredibly kind, and Cilvaringz rapidly became something of a pet project. She and RZA's uncle
Vince, who Cilvaringz had also managed to track down, were
both surprisingly understanding—which just goes to show how
the right energy can infuse even the most suspect situations. For
whatever reason, he had made an impression and the goodwill
was strong, so between the two of them, they flagged up certain events RZA might be at so Cilvaringz could fly over from
Holland, occupy the pavement outside them, and do his thing.
And yet somehow, RZA continued to elude this increasingly
sophisticated manhunt.

On his fifth trip, Cilvaringz finally got his hands on the loca-
tion of Razor Sharp Records, where RZA had an office. Feeling the hope rising, he installed himself back at the YMCA, put
together a fresh presentation package, and set off to 99 University Place. A wonderfully fitting address for a student in search
of a teacher. RZA was going to walk past at some point. He
HAD to. Unless there was an underground secret entrance or
some shit. Fuck it—it was the best lead he had.

On the first day he dug in outside the offices, Cilvaringz met
nearly the entire Wu-Tang Clan . . . except RZA. Laying a copy
of his demo on each of them, he settled back in for the long
haul with just one demo banked in his pocket. But as they left,
who should come strolling past . . . no, not RZA, but his sister
Sophia.

Exchanging some doorstep pleasantries and affectionately

intrigued by what fresh level of psychosis Cilvaringz had now reached, she cut straight to the chase. She hadn't found any dead squirrels outside her house with lyrics pinned to them, so maybe he wasn't actually dangerous. Breaking into a smile, she invited him upstairs.

The floor was bustling with activity, not least a delegation from Quentin Tarantino who had come to discuss the music for *Kill Bill*. Everyone seemed to have a place and a purpose, but Cilvaringz was entering under royal protection. His savior strode over to the tape deck, put in Cilvaringz's demo, and cranked it as loud as it would go to gauge the reactions of everyone there while Ringz scanned a wall decorated with a thousand different phone numbers. Surely one had to be RZA's current digits.

Just as he finally pinpointed the Abbot's number and was sidling over with a pen, Sophia began whipping up the assembled throng. Shit—if ever a priceless piece of PR was done, she was killing it.

"Who dis?" people began to ask. " 'S'all right," they began to say. "Yo, this is dope." Whether they were just being polite to RZA's sister or for real, Cilvaringz was past caring. This was some proper movie shit already. The phone rang and Cilvaringz's first instinct was bitter disappointment as the volume was scythed down and it looked like his fifteen seconds might be over.

It was Ghostface Killah. And he was calling from jail. He probably wanted to shoot the breeze with his homies and see how things were lining up for his release, but he barely got started before Cilvaringz's fairy godmother took control and played his demo into the phone. And despite it hijacking precious prison phone minutes, Ghost was digging it.

Step back. Who was to say Tarantino wasn't directing this

very scene? After everything he'd been through, Cilvaringz was watching his demo being played over the phone to one of the biggest rappers in the world, who was listening to it from jail and stamping it with his seal of approval. Fuck knows what Ghost had really made of the whole thing, he'd been bum-rushed in no uncertain terms, but if someone at his level was prepared to go with it, then that was already enough. It was a wonderfully surreal moment of catharsis.

The second he hung up, Sophia hammered the keys on the dial pad. Someone answered. "Yo, Bobby—you gotta get down here. That guy who's been sending you all those demos and letters and lyrics and shit? He's here at Razor, everyone's loving his demo, Ghost—everyone, and you need to be here right now."

She rang off. "RZA's on his way."

The minutes scratched by in agony. This was it. This was what it had all been about. The Abbot had granted him an audience and he was on his way.

At long last, the mercurial figure of RZA swept in. "Peace." He didn't break stride until he was in his office and the door had swung shut. Seconds later, the sub-bass on Cilvaringz's demo could be heard rattling the walls. He must have listened to about half of it before the door opened once more and the Abbot beckoned the journeyman in. Ahead of Tarantino's people and everything. Was this all a cruel dream?

RZA sat there in silence with his fingertips together. You could cut the atmosphere with a dagger. The silence continued. Cilvaringz began to shift nervously in his seat. After what seemed like a couple of centuries, RZA finally spoke.

"I've got all your demos and your letters, and here it is. I don't think you're that great a rapper just yet, but under the guidance of the Wu-Tang Generals I think we may have something. I'm going to assign you to the label just because your motivation and determination shines through. Here's my phone number and my address—come over to the house later and we'll talk."

The temple door had swung ajar.

FOUNDATIONS

"Walk around New York and write what you see. Write what you hear. Write what you feel. And then let's talk some more."

Cilvaringz hadn't been sure what to expect. In fact, now that he thought about it, he hadn't actually given any focus whatsoever to what might happen after he finally met RZA. For months, the one and only goal had been to track him down, and now that he had swept triumphantly over the finish line, his eyes were adjusting to the terrain. It was like having climbed the highest mountain imaginable, then breaking through the clouds to see a whole new range of peaks.

He had, of course, spent weeks walking around New York already, though with every sense revolving around that one mission. Now the challenge would be to immerse himself back into the mayhem with an empty mind. He put in a few days of disjointed observation, then reluctantly remembered that he had unfinished business back in Holland.

He was nearing the end of his degree in entertainment law, and with only a matter of months to go until graduation, he struggled over whether to ride the wave for all he was worth or go back, finish what he had started, and then rejoin the path. Every last person he knew thought he was fucking insane to return to provincial Holland from the gates of Shaolin. Every last person, that is, except RZA, who respected that steely sense of responsibility in the face of a shimmering dream. Who the hell hunts down the Wu over continents and then says, actually, can you hang on a bit—I need to go and finish college? But it demonstrated a solid head and a grasp of the big picture, and if anything, it cemented his place in RZA's mind as he took his leave.

On May 26, 1999, two years to the day since ODB had pulled him up onstage in Amsterdam, Cilvaringz walked tentatively up to the door of the Wu Villa in Paris and rang the bell. Paris was the temporary hub for RZA's international operations and HQ for the new label Cilvaringz had been signed to. He knew he was there to ink a contract, but hadn't anticipated that within minutes, he and RZA would be in the studio together working on their first collaboration—a track called "Ninja Starz." It was the opening salvo for the solo album he had just signed for, and with RZA helming production and Cilvaringz rapping, the track swiftly came together to lay a foundation for the journey ahead. There's nothing like an injection of instant gratification to hit the ground running—it lifts you out of the workmanlike duty to the blank page so many artists feel in the wilderness, and as he left to write the rest of his album, he was rushing on a high.

For the next few years, as he built, tweaked, tore down, and rebuilt his solo album, Cilvaringz drew all his inspiration from the Wu-Tang idea space. The only problem was, that wasn't his reality. His touchstones were largely derivative, drawing on a shiny but ultimately shallow array of swords, guillotines, darts, temples, and mystical-sounding kung fu shit. When RZA had said to him on that first day, go out and write what you see, he had been trying to encourage Cilvaringz to find his own voice, his own mirror to the inner and outer worlds. But as a young Wu fan signed to a Wu label, Cilvaringz saw his job as adding another harmony to an existing philosophy.

How many rock bands copied the Stones or Aerosmith before they found their own sound? How many acoustic folk bands started off with Dylan covers before their own identity matured? And Cilvaringz began in exactly the same bubble, using slang out of context, harnessing the imagery but not the meaning, and basically trying to out Wu-Tang the Clan in a bid for acceptance and a desire to make the grade.

But while his music hadn't yet started to sing in key, Cilvaringz was a shrewd motherfucker. That course in entertainment law hadn't been some teenage "I don't know what to do with my life so I'll go to college till I figure it out" cliché. Born to a Moroccan immigrant family, the values instilled in him at an early age had generated a sense of personal responsibility, hard work, and self-reliance, and those guiding principles had been embedded deep enough for him to know he needed a practical trade as well as a dream. If his unlikely ascent to the heights of the rap game was an outside shot at best, then he would lay the foundation for a livelihood elsewhere within the industry. Graduating that summer, he had one last major project before he was free to shoot the moon, safe in the knowledge that he hadn't burned any bridges. That graduation project was wonderfully amorphous; it could involve anything that fell under the reassuringly broad umbrella of entertainment law. So what—an internship being bitched good and proper in a law firm, making tea for Z-list celebrities and kowtowing to a budget Ari Gold? Fuck that. Let's book a world tour for RZA.

You could see how this made all kinds of sense from Cilvaringz's perspective. It was two fat juicy birds with one slab of concrete. He would get extraordinary experience at the sharp end of the industry, learn the ropes for real, meet promoters, lawyers, venue owners, label executives, A&R men, unattainable women, rappers, and movie stars—all the while seeing the world in style alongside RZA. It also set him apart from the other, perhaps more talented rappers that RZA brought up through the ranks, as he was offering more than just rhymes—he was proving himself multi-faceted and capable across a broader spectrum. It was an incredible opportunity.

The really astonishing thing was that RZA agreed. He was actually going to let this kid run his world tour. Either the character of Bobby Digital was running rampant across the RZA's better judgment, or he really saw something in Cilvaringz, enough to gamble his own tour on—not just a flimsy recording contract and a few days of studio production. It was a signal honor, a mark of faith, and a show of respect.

RZA's dictatorship of the Clan had ended a couple of years previously, and while nothing would ever change the family bonds, he was enjoying his own liberation. He no longer took the responsibility for it all on his shoulders, and the Bobby Digital persona symbolized his own break for freedom. To take on a whole new alter ego and actually live it day by day instead of only when the cameras were rolling spoke volumes about his reaction to those high-pressure, high-intensity years. It wasn't even enough to go solo—he needed to experience life through a whole different set of eyes, a new prism of perception channeled through new mediums of expression.

And part of that was being answerable only to himself. If he wanted someone no one had ever heard of to run his tour, then fuck it—that's what was gonna happen. And when Cilvaringz put himself forward as the opening act, RZA took one look at the work he was putting in at the coalface and how he was progressing in the studio . . . and agreed. So hold up: Cilvaringz had gone from a wing and a prayer to tour agent, tour manager, AND opening act . . . Maybe God didn't play dice, but destiny was clearing out the casino.

One hundred sixty-three cities in fifty-six countries. Bit overboard for a graduation project, don't you think?

The pace was punishing. Between the traveling, the back-to-back performances, the endless headfuck as deals changed, promoters fell through, venues collapsed, hotels lost bookings, and money zigzagged across continents, Cilvaringz almost forgot to take it all in and enjoy himself. These are the moments in life where you need to stop, look around, and pay homage to the fact that you're in Hong Kong playing a sold-out show with your illustrious mentor and not working nine to five in a creased suit somewhere in Holland. But he had put himself under so much pressure that the days, the time zones, and the memories flew by without a moment of clarity—there was just way too much to do.

Somewhere along a very blurry ride, the two of them were sitting in a Stuttgart apartment when the subject of Egypt cropped up. Neither of them had ever been, it wasn't featured on the first stretch of the tour schedule, and both had it on the bucket list. Nothing much came of it beyond RZA asking Cilvaringz whether he'd like to come with him if he ever went. Within minutes, the subject melted away into something altogether more practical, and it seemed but a tiny footnote to the years spent on tour together. That is, until 2004, when Cilvaringz's phone rang and RZA said, "Pack a bag. We're going to Egypt."

RZA sent him his ticket and the two met in Cairo before working their way down to the Giza plateau and the Mena House Hotel, an old royal hunting lodge that lay directly in the shadow of the pyramids. No other hotel in Giza lay so close to the ancient site, boasted such commanding views, or was quite so luxurious. They interviewed several potential guides, most of whom were more anxious to guide them to the gift shop than a holistic understanding of the Old Kingdom, but just as disillusion began to set in, they stumbled across a very different kind of fellow: a gentleman named Hossam. Steeped in Egyptology and with a natural-born instinct to teach, Hossam beguiled them with historical anecdotes, contextual illumination, and animated insight into Egyptian culture. Oh, and he was also seriously well connected, something that became fascinatingly evident as he invited them into the pyramids after closing time.

It was like a cross between Indiana Wu and Lawrence of Shaolin as they galloped toward the horizon on horseback. The whole windswept stallion vibe was in full effect as their turbans fluttered in the breeze and their scimitars glinted in the sunset . . .

Okay, I made up the turbans and scimitar bit. They wobbled their way toward Orion's titans, dismounted dustily, and stepped into the crucible of history.

From tomb to tomb, from sandstorm to sandstorm, they entered the original chambers of death. Hossam took them on a unique journey past locked doors and fenced-off archaeological digs, burrowing into the stone and opening rooms only a handful of academics had seen in the past three thousand years. And then, on their final night, they rode back to the pyramids at sunset and climbed Khufu. The pyramids lend themselves to an easy climb; since their covering fell victim to the winds, the outer bones of the structure are effectively a huge set of steps. Leaping from hewn boulder to limestone tablet, RZA and Cilvaringz got about halfway up before sitting down and gazing out over time, space, and silent ritual. Eternity rushed in.

As they sat, heads bowed to the dynasty that demanded such immortality and the forgotten craftsmen who forged it, they marveled at the precision, the detail, the skill, the art, and above all the permanence. Cilvaringz might not have had that panoramic moment of reflection and meditative appreciation on the world tour, but here on the pillars of time, the third eye opened.

"Someday, we need to do something together that lasts through the ages," whispered Cilvaringz.

RZA nodded, lost in thought. Shape-shifting in the lone and level sands . . . "Word."

No pressure then.

SHAOLIN SCHOOL

The debut Cilvaringz album finally hit the shelves in 2007. It had been through umpteen incarnations, and the pendulum had swung back and forth on two key factors. Somewhere around the 2004 mark, his lyrical ideas came of age, and looking back at the curiously hollow reams of ninja-ass swordfights he had written, he realized that much of it was essentially meaningless.

On the one hand, he felt that he had a lot to say lyrically but that so far, he hadn't said any of it. Looking at the page with a critical eye, he knew that there was more derivation than inspiration woven into the words, and, taking a deep breath, he tore up the entire lyrical framework to start afresh in his own voice. And yet on the other hand, his production had made the leap from derivation to inspiration. He had finally grasped the secret of the beats—and while heavy drums, big samples, and gritty sonics might sound Wu, there was a reason that they never could be.

The breakthrough dawned in London. RZA was filming *Derailed* there, and with a suitably roomy apartment at his disposal, it seemed rude not to pay a visit. Every day for three weeks, RZA would head to the set for a long day's filming while Cilvaringz stayed behind and dug through his crates. RZA had a mobile studio with him based around an Akai MPC sampling and sequencing unit, and having access to that allowed Cilvaringz to analyze the mechanics of his production. Within the MPC was the geometry of Wu, the start and end points of samples, the layering of drums, the core elements of a loop broken down. By day Cilvaringz would explore the parameters and by night he would watch RZA make music, until the combination of the two insights yielded the most unexpected epiphany.

RZA reveled in small glitches as long as he was in the zone when they occurred. You can trim a loop to the perfect nanometer if you spend long enough tweaking it, but by the time you've finished ironing out the creases, you've inadvertently sanitized the vibe. You can pick the "right" sound to underpin a bass line, but if you trust your instincts and pick the "wrong" one, you create a far more powerful conduit for musical energy. A magnetic dissonance dissolving into a golden ratio.

There's a very fine line between the sublime and the ridiculous, and RZA's genius was to ride it like a samurai surfing. Again and again, what sounded like a mistake in a string sample or a vocal sample actually gave a loop a whole different dimension of natural life when the drums and bass came in on top. Had it all been broken down and wiped clean, the loop would sound almost identical, but it wouldn't have that intangible spark that made it magic. What RZA was effectively doing was introducing a wild card, a rogue element that strayed outside the lines and infused the beats with realness—a feel more redolent of a live jam than studio mathematics. It was a very Eastern counterpoint to a very Western technology—letting the spirit flow free rather than trying to reconstruct it through dry logic.

The secret was spontaneity, the imperfection that creates true perfection. Beauty works in exactly the same way: a beautiful woman or a handsome man so often has a slight quirk that makes them mesmerizing. Perhaps an oddly shaped nose, which taken alone may seem bizarre, but when set within the face as a whole, lifts it from magazine beauty to real beauty. And if that nose were ever operated on to make it officially "perfect," the face would lose its mysterious allure. It was about embracing a world outside binary code—letting nature and inspiration breathe rather than stuffing them into a corset. And it was about seeing the grand design, how different elements come together as one to make a whole far greater than the sum of its parts. That was a game changer for Cilvaringz. It wasn't a technique, it was a philosophy.

Even as he made the breakthrough, Cilvaringz was examining his own rapping and realizing how clinical it sounded. He no longer felt free on a microphone; perhaps it was the idea of releasing a documented version rather than just freestyling that made him seize up, but as he listened, he was effectively tendering his resignation to the rap game. It wasn't fun anymore, it wasn't natural anymore, and he was overthinking his vocals into flatness. He felt that his album had been well received because the Clan members guesting on it had brought it to life, but as he reflected on his journey and wondered what to do next, he began to revise his ambitions.

He was never going to be the greatest rapper—if for no other reason than that he didn't feel totally comfortable spitting rhymes. He was proud that he had finally developed his own lyrical voice, and that side of the album did speak from the heart, but he was no longer confident that he was the person to bring those thoughts to a beat. Looking at the music he was making, he suddenly began to wonder what various beats he'd rapped over himself might sound like on, say, a Raekwon album or an Inspectah Deck album. He felt that his production had far more to say for itself than his voice, and that the sound he was starting to capture was akin to the Wu-Tang sound of the nineties.

RZA was taking a keen interest in the development of Cilvaringz's production. There was a real yin and yang going on, as one of RZA's mantras had always been "A man must evolve." So even as Cilvaringz began to harness the sound of classic Wu, RZA himself was moving away from it toward new challenges, new textures, and new musical horizons. He wouldn't make the kind of beats Cilvaringz was sending him himself, but he was intrigued to hear so much of his own essence coming through. Even as RZA moved on from his old sound, Cilvaringz was picking up the mantle and firing it back at him, and the Abbot couldn't help but be drawn to the flame.

As far as Cilvaringz was concerned, there was still so much great music to be made in that original Wu-Tang style. And furthermore, he was convinced that what the fans, himself included, wanted above all was more albums from that sonic lineage. The rest of the Clan were experimenting with more contemporary sounds, but Cilvaringz was convinced that if an environment could be created where he could write raw, Shaolin-sounding beats for the Clan to go in heavy on, he would be able to evoke a spirit in them that they were accessing less and less with new-generation beats. He wondered to himself what might happen if another album were made in the original style. It was a profoundly seductive vision.

It was still something of a chimera, though. In the meantime, he would focus his production energies on a different project, an album for one of the most electric Wu-Tang affiliates, Killah Priest. His first album, *Heavy Mental,* had been anchored in grand themes, channeling biblical imagery into a modern matrix, and as Cilvaringz gazed at the mountains and kasbahs that surrounded him, he felt that they might make a perfect team.

Writing beat after beat, he hunkered down in the plains of Morocco and began shaping a dreamscape. But it wasn't meant to be. Scheduling issues and the fact that he and Killah Priest were on different continents and in different time zones took their toll. Over the subsequent months, the communication lapses and their differing rhythms of life spiraled, and it became clear to them both that this particular moment in time wasn't providential. But Cilvaringz was determined to bring his beats to life, and with that project hitting the wall, he went back to RZA and asked him what he thought the best move might be.

RZA's movie career was picking up steam and he was in a totally different zone from Cilvaringz musically. He couldn't see any direct involvement for himself at that stage, but he had an underlying sense that his protégé might be onto something. He made a suggestion that could have gone nowhere, the kind of move that gives a project just enough oxygen to breathe if it was meant to be and not enough to sustain it if it wasn't.

"Forget albums, end goals, release dates, and finished products" was his advice. "Just make music, bring in all the Clan, all the most talented Wu affiliates, and let's see where it goes. Who knows if it will ever come to anything, but if this is what your heart is telling you to do, go do it. And keep me in the loop."

It was a very tall order. No label was going to invest in recording music for its own sake. The Clan were busy, and if he wanted them to record, then he was going to have to pay them. Cilvaringz didn't have the money to invest himself, and it would take hundreds of thousands of dollars to see this through properly. But what was a label beyond investment, publicity, and distribution anyway? Why couldn't a private investor supply the funding and then they could cross the other bridges as they came?

The simple answer to that was that a private investor would be even less enthusiastic about plowing money into an open-ended project. It was the antithesis of a business plan, with no guarantee of a return or even an end point. But with RZA backing him on paper, he explored his options and finally stumbled across Mr. S, the man I occasionally did some consulting for. Mr. S was a businessman through and through, but he was also something of a romantic. A few hundred thousand wasn't going to dent his portfolio, but it made almost no financial sense to invest. Swayed by Cilvaringz's passion and heavily influenced by his son, who was a huge Wu fan, he finally agreed on terms that were simultaneously draconian and absurdly indulgent. He would fund the development stage, but if the music never reached a point where it could recoup the investment, Cilvaringz signed into a repayment plan from his own pocket, where failure would mean working for ten years or more to square the debt. It was a huge gamble.

The more he thought about the responsibility he was about to take on and the years of work he was about to invest, the more concerned he grew about the album making a weeklong splash and then disappearing into the annals of semi-anonymity. By 2007–8, the pattern in the music business was already pretty well carved, and Cilvaringz racked his brain for a way to make it stand out. The single-copy idea that he had hinted at to me in 2007 remained nothing more than a fanciful notion, but by 2009 and the Biennale in Marrakech, he had begun to give it more serious thought. The experience of running a citywide art exhibition had brought the differing perceptions of art and music kicking and screaming to the forefront, and he was searching for a way to bring back that halo effect of "art" to the world of music. Was it presentation? Was it rarity? Was it price? Or was it just bullshit?

He developed the concept further before floating to RZA the idea of a single-copy album presented as a work of art. As they discussed it, neither was totally convinced or totally against the idea, and they weren't anywhere near that stage yet anyway— you couldn't preempt such a radical fate without knowing what the music sounded like first. But they did settle on one move. If it ever did come to a single-copy album, security would be critical, as one leak would reduce the whole thing to farce. So just in case they decided to go down that road, they should embed antileak protections into the entire recording process, so that the option remained live. And with that in mind . . . the recording began.

It wasn't *Once Upon a Time in Shaolin*. It wasn't a Wu-Tang Clan album. It wasn't a Cilvaringz album. It wasn't anything at all. It was a series of recordings—an open-ended experiment that would seal its own fate.

ONE IN THE CHAMBER

It all began inside out. The first move was to establish a series of chapters that would hone the identity of the album. An idea, a name, an image, and a motif were laid down for each song before the music was made in their spirit. It was about creating a soundscape for each title, figuring out which emcee would breathe the right life into it, and working from overarching imagery to full sonic complexity.

As the narrative began to take shape, the Clan began to sculpt the album's multiple threads into vivid frequency. Opinions were sharply divided about the musical direction that the beats had taken. Some members like Raekwon, Masta Killa, and Ghostface thrived on the rugged, lo-fi grooves that landed, savoring the opportunity to revisit their roots, while others like Inspectah Deck and U-God remained unconvinced that such a style could work in today's world. Hip-hop was a far smoother, shinier place than it had been twenty years ago, and half the Clan were uncomfortable moving backward rather than forward. Some even described it as "funeral music," insisting that today's ear would want little to do with this kind of aesthetic.

And yet as the recording sessions advanced, it was becoming clear that many of the Clan sounded different. It wasn't a question of better or worse, it was about their vocal reaction to the aggressive beats. There was a note of urgency and rebellion, even tinges of anger driving the flows, and as RZA got ears on the session recordings, he was intrigued by the subtle shifts of energy. It was a strange feeling, not quite coming full circle, but orbiting the core on a new trajectory.

Despite the responsibilities he had taken on in other arenas, RZA kept gravitating back to his oversight role on the project, and with each iteration, he got more involved. It began in broad strokes with directorial prompts, but before long he was homing in on arrangement sequences, edits, tweaks, and hands-on production when he felt the mark had been missed or when he could see an extra 10 percent hiding between the bars. As more and more artists came on, including key Wu-Tang affiliates and Redman, the sweep through the extended Wu family and the classic sonic nexus all began to point in one direction. It was ever more apparent to RZA that however this project had begun, it was now sounding unmistakably like a Wu-Tang Clan album.

He was hesitant to make any kind of declaration to that effect, though. He wanted to keep his options open before fully committing the Wu name, and he was also aware that certain frictions and relationships he had with the Clan might actually damage the album's momentum. If he stepped in too heavy, there might be a sudden wave of family dispute, but without any declaration that this was an official Wu-Tang album, everybody just focused on getting the music nailed rather than the additional meaning and pressure of stamping the W on it. So he decided to take on a more extensive role behind the scenes and see where the rhymes landed. Monthly conferences between Cilvaringz and RZA morphed into weekly and then almost daily as it neared completion.

Skits began to be written for the album, and a cast of gloriously unlikely characters stepped in to play a role. Barcelona soccer players were miked up to play lost Spanish tourists after coming backstage at a Catalan concert, and Carice van Houten, the Red Witch in *Game of Thrones,* also took a cameo role. Shit, even I recorded a few lines as an overexcited TV reporter covering the Wu-Tang heist of the World Bank. And then, of course, there was the least likely of all: Cher.

Cher had proved unbelievably cool. So often in this world, midlevel artists are surrounded by a phalanx of attitude-heavy managers, agents, publicists, and assistants while the undisputed stars got over themselves a while back and are disarmingly human. So it proved with Cher, who didn't want any money, didn't throw up any hoops to jump through, and sent back several versions of each section with the humility and professionalism of a true artist. The only regret with Cher was not having had the balls to ask her to appear more on the record, but with her not accepting any payment and her being Cher, Cilvaringz was very wary of abusing her goodwill. She kept offering, but you never want to outstay your welcome or ask what else is in the sack when you've just been handed a present.

It was a voyage back through the original chambers, interpreted by a producer for whom that sound had proved life changing and guided by the Abbot who had created it in the first place. Each rapper had revisited a part of himself, a part of their shared experience, and a strand of hip-hop history. It was a last hurrah for a seminal sound, and the record felt more and more like an artifact than a new album. And so came the title, *Once Upon a Time in Shaolin,* encapsulating that window of memory— far too searing for nostalgia alone, but strangely isolated in today's world. It almost felt like it belonged buried under the desert sands rather than in a record store. A very volatile time capsule.

It had begun life in abstract form, and if there had ever been a defined goal behind it, that mission had been to give the fans a final chance to revisit an epoch. But from inception to completion, an awful lot had changed in the music industry. The downward spiral of sales, appreciation, and value had grown exponentially quicker, and after six years in the making, both Cilvaringz and RZA grew increasingly disillusioned by the album's potential fate. Especially Cilvaringz. RZA had his legacy etched in stone, but for Cilvaringz, this was his magnum opus and he despaired at the thought of a fortnight in the sun before disappearing into respectful oblivion. It had gotten to the point where musical quality almost didn't matter; even the greatest albums of any given year tended to gravitate toward the realms of amnesia within weeks or months. What could they do to set it apart, to make it special?

The impact of the Marrakech Biennale weighed heavy on Cilvaringz's mind, how some arts were on a pedestal while others, like music, remained bound by diminishing value. In the years since the one-copy concept was first broached, RZA had seen the disparity between perceptions of art and perceptions of music widen, and even as he moved further into the film sphere, he suffered constant pangs about the state of the music world. Until one night as they discussed where the hi-hat should come in on a song, the conversation turned back to the single-copy concept.

2

This album felt different from a normal new release anyway, and if that overriding sense of it as an artifact prevailed, then perhaps this was the perfect work to use in a statement about art, music, and value.

As they went backward and forward on such a momentous decision, the heavens began to nudge them in the ribs. Nipsey Hussle sprang up with his hundred-dollar mixtape and Jay Z came with his #NewRules campaign. The planets seemed to be aligning for a radical move. Back in 2007, the omens were all wrong for so extreme an idea, but in 2013, the environment had changed beyond recognition. If ever there was a time to do it . . . that time was now. #Norules.

Cilvaringz didn't know how to feel. He wanted this album to take a historic course, perhaps even something that could aspire to that moment he and RZA had shared on the Great Pyramid. But on the other hand, what if nobody ever heard it and his six years of work ended up shrouded in desirable mystique but not a lot else? What musician doesn't want the world to hear his record?

And then there was the question of the fans to whom he had been faithfully promising an old-school album. He'd been hyping every inch of the album's progress to the die-hard supporters on the Clan's official Web forum. Mainlining their enthusiasm to feed his inspiration and perhaps even to talk himself out of the single-copy idea, he was only too aware that he had raised expectations to fever pitch. How would they feel about the rug being pulled from under them?

If he and RZA decided to go for it, it would be a sacrifice on the altar of symbolism. There was every chance that the music might not be properly heard, but if we as a society had arrived at this point where musicians felt so undermined by the lack of value placed on their work, perhaps someone needed to play devil's advocate and paint a dystopian picture of the future. It would challenge preconceptions about art; it would create an aura around a piece of music; it would restore drama, anticipation, and mystique while reclaiming the power of artists to shape their music's future. It would explore ideas about whether music was a right or a privilege, act as a wake-up call to piracy, and symbolically reattach value to a piece of music, however extreme the means might be.

But above all, it would start a debate. And that would prove more valuable than the music itself. This wasn't a solution, who knew if it was a viable business model, but it would undeniably trigger arguments and soul-searching in equal measure—both among the people who made the album and the people who wanted to hear it. It wasn't an answer. It was a question.

As if to confirm the theory about the link between economic and experiential value, a scientific approach was taken by Cilvaringz in a short aside known as the Bundle Experiments. Four limited-edition digital packs of unreleased music were created and priced at different points—$50, $100, $150, and $200 respectively—all with different tracks in them. The question was, would a higher financial outlay affect people's willingness to leak the music onto the Internet, and could it be proven, at least on a micro level, that price affected piracy? Sure enough, the two cheaper packs leaked almost instantly, but the two more expensive ones are yet to leak. It wasn't conclusive, but it certainly played a role in bolstering the single-copy idea.

Finally, after a hurricane of oscillating uncertainty, the die was cast. But if it was going to be done, it was going to be done properly. It would have to utilize the formal framework of the art world to make a statement and be sold by an art auction house. And it had to be special on every level; you couldn't just hand over a plastic CD cover. Everything had to be lavish perfection without falling into the bling trap.

As RZA and Cilvaringz made the decision, another person who needed a heads-up was Mr. S. He sounded genuinely excited about the prospect, and it was that very night that I received his phone call. I wasn't really there to manage his investment or to try and manage anyone involved—I was there to give a perspective. I wasn't forced on anyone, either; once Cilvaringz got over the shock that the guy he'd met a few times and who was actually on the album because of his shouty British accent also had ties to Mr. S, it seemed more like cosmic synchronicity than an interloper from the investor's camp.

If Mr. S had been appointing someone to militantly watch his money, it sure as hell wouldn't have been me. He didn't get to where he was without having an eye for who and what would fit a project, and this was no exception. It all felt like fate. RZA and I met by lengthy phone call so he could approve or reject my joining the board, and by the time we said our good nights, there was an instinctive depth of trust that boded well for the hard road ahead.

There was only ever one man who could create the casing. Yahya had already attained legendary status in Morocco as one of the king's favorite designers, and recent years had seen royal families and grand hotels throughout the world embrace his unique style. Distilling the intricacies of Moorish geometry through a crisp, contemporary vortex, he combined dazzling detail and futuristic spins on classicism with craftsmanship reminiscent of a golden age. In short, he was a fucking don when it came to metalwork and the perfect artist to cast the album in befitting majesty.

As several nesting boxes were crafted with microscopic saws just millimeters long, Cilvaringz's next idea was to riff on the sleeve notes. Instead of a short booklet, a 174-page book was printed on parchment, then bound in leather and gilded by a master Serbian bookbinder, aLexLibris. Inside were the lyrics, a drawing to emblematize each track, as well as a series of anecdotes about the album's development and narrative scope.

If *Once Upon a Time in Shaolin* was a journey back through time and felt more like an archaeological discovery than a current album, and if the skills used to create its physical incarnation were almost lost to the modern world, then the historical parallels to a single-copy album began to crystallize. Recording may be a modern invention, but the commissioning of sheet music had a long pedigree, and of course painting and sculpture were primarily sold to or commissioned by one patron alone. This was, as CNN senior vice president Ron Ciccone quipped about the album, the commission system in reverse. Instead of receiving a commission and creating the work accordingly, the artist would create the work and then commission a buyer. Echoes of the Renaissance, the Baroque, and the Enlightenment bustled in alongside the antique dream of a lost treasure.

Elevating hip-hop to a formally recognized standing within the elite art world. Putting hip-hop culture on the same stage as a Picasso or a Rembrandt. Having the self-belief and self-confidence to know hip-hop belongs there, not merely believe it or hope it—but know it. If all else failed, then we had planted a flag at the summit of "art" as society labeled it. It wasn't even a play or a heist on the art world—*Once Upon a Time in Shaolin* belonged there by right as a representative of every rapper, every poet, and every DJ who had ever rocked the block. It was a work of art. Period.

If we were going to announce a sole existing copy of an album, adorned in an arklike casing, and successfully negotiate it through the ivy-strewn pathways of the art world, we were going to have to be damn sure that we could hold our own, or we would be torn apart. You wondered whether anyone would want us to succeed, whether the music world would view the whole thing as an exercise in hubris and whether the art world would dismiss it as pretention.

The fans would be outraged; there would be cries of "Music for the people, Wu-Tang for the children"; the group would be accused of any number of travesties from cultural vandalism to C.R.E.A.M. sellouts, but as I got deeper into the concept with Cilvaringz and RZA, my own reservations ebbed away. If it was ever to be done, these were the guys to do it. Everyone was aware of the risks and rewards, and no one was full of shit. Had I sensed even a fraction of this project was too far up its own ass, I would have walked, but the more I got to know who I was dealing with, the more I wholeheartedly believed that this had to be done—for better or for worse.

And thus arrived the moment of truth. The Clan had to vote on it.

There was of course, a "full and frank exchange of ideas." Some felt that they had been misled about the nature of the project and others instinctively recoiled at the idea of a single-copy sale to the highest bidder. But as the conversations continued, they came to understand why things had played out in the way that they had, and having all suffered the debilitating effects of the music industry crisis in equal measure, they united behind the concept. Many still held reservations, and it was a big fucking ask, to allow their names and reputations to stand or fall with this lunatic-sounding project, but it was now or never. Someone would step up to challenge the status quo at some point, and Wu-Tang had always been on the leading edge of musical, cultural, and business innovation. No one was sure; you'd have to be crazy to be totally convinced, but everyone was down with letting it play.

Time to bring the ruckus.

THE QUICKENING

The album was locked and loaded. The serpentine silver swirls sparkled in the twilight. We were ready to ride the riptide.

Piling irony onto paradox, we needed a digital home for this most analog of ideas. I learned long ago that contradictions are the crucible of creativity, where yin and yang, light and dark, good and evil whirl together like the dervishes of lucidity. Dualism is the electricity of the human soul, where staggering complexity traces back to twin poles of energy in perpetual motion.

It's a funny one. Digitality is a binary representation of reality, a spectrum of sensory experience forged from the interplay of 1s and 0s. It still blows my mind to listen to a piece of music or gaze at a mesmerizing photograph and think that what I'm really hearing or seeing is a sequence of 1s and 0s. Who knew the mathematics of being and the fabric of reality could be broken down to a pattern consisting of only two primary elements? But then again, DNA—the entire blueprint of life—breaks down to a sequence of just four elements. The relationship between simplicity and complexity was yet another nod to polarity, and you had to ask yourself, if pure sonic experience can be broken down into 1s and 0s, what did that say about consciousness and the abstraction of emotion? Maybe trying to reconcile the mechanics of soul with our experience of it was the ultimate proof that magic exists.

So while we were fighting the fallout of the digital revolution, the battle had nothing to do with its literal definition. The arguments that rage over whether a slice of vinyl could trump a .wav file or whether a Moog synthesizer could sing a warmer bass note than a virtual synth were a million miles away from the statement we were hoping to make. It wasn't a Luddite rearguard action to defy progress and wallow in nostalgia; this had nothing to do with the technology and everything to do with our perceptions of value, society, and ultimately, ourselves.

Now check this out: "According to Nielsen SoundScan, which collects recorded-music sales information, of the eight million unique digital tracks sold in 2011, 94 percent—7.5 million tracks—sold fewer than one hundred units, and an astonishing 32 percent sold only one copy." Thanks to music analyst and critic Bob Lefsetz for painting such a stark picture.

Maybe 94 percent of the tracks were just fucking terrible? Or maybe there was just so much great music out there with no way of raising its head above the parapet that no one even knew it existed. Maybe we were drowning in an embarrassment of riches.

Electronic music was an autonomous zone of democratized creativity. You didn't need years of formal musical training, you needed instinct and intuition. With samplers entering the equation, the world was at our fingertips; with some funky breaks, a drum machine, a synth or two, and a heavyweight flow, anyone with unpolished talent could make music. It was like taking a sledgehammer to a glass ceiling, a musical leveler that brought the street onto the radar and made self-expression a real possibility. So much of the greatest music we have been blessed with was born of struggle and hardship, from the blues to hip-hop, and having the tools to shape a cultural voice was a profound evolution. The playing field was looking a lot more level, and subcultures had a lot more control over the game being played.

As the millennium drew near, things began to snowball in a new and unforeseen direction, driven once more by emergent technology. To be a bedroom producer in 1990, you needed about five thousand dollars for decent equipment. Five thousand dollars tended to be affordable if you were really determined, but it was still five thousand dollars. Compared to a wardrobe-sized synth, or to years of musical training, it was a liberating price tag, but only for those who saw raising that kind of money as a challenge on the way to realizing a dream.

As personal computing technology accelerated at breakneck pace, suddenly it was becoming possible to buy a laptop, download some cracked software, and do everything in the box for a thousand dollars or less. Moreover, people who weren't necessarily intent on becoming producers would install music software and fuck around with it for fun. Suddenly the numbers of people producing music went through the roof. A triumph for democratization, surely?

The same went for actually releasing music. Eight hundred dollars to press up five hundred records was still eight hundred dollars, and that was even before you took into consideration the man-hours of pavement pounding between record shops to get your profile off the ground and angle for a label deal. It was eminently doable, but you had to be pretty motivated to actually do it. With the rise of digital formats and the extraordinary connectivity of the Internet, it quickly became possible to put your music out for next to nothing. Another barrier removed.

Here we had the natural progression of the democratization that had been such a key factor in the birth of underground electronic music. Money was now virtually no barrier to production, and surely the Internet and the MP3 would finally eradicate major labels from the equation and create a global musical subculture where open-source dynamics and digital freedoms would forge ever more independent models.

So what happened? The removal of physicality from music somehow began to devalue it as something lasting and intrinsically substantial. MP3s slowly became transient and disposable, without people—your author included—really being aware of that subtle shift in perception. Anthems with life spans of many months dwindled to a few weeks and then often into obscurity. With investment filters vanishing, people who made music no longer had to take a long hard look at a track before releasing it, as there was nothing to lose by putting it out digitally.

Democratization began to leak away into saturation as it became virtually impossible to wade through every new release to try and find a hidden gem. Rather than twenty tracks per subgenre per week, thousands began to clog the pathways. Drowning in a sea of white noise.

As the democratization of production and distribution spiraled from a utopian ideal into a dystopian sea of digital overload, the sustainability of independent music plummeted. With such an intimidating quantity of music out there, the focus started to become as much about presentation as musical substance. It simply wasn't good enough anymore to make great music and trust distribution channels to ensure it got heard. Independent record labels with limited promotional budgets were subsumed in the new economic realities, and corporate entities seemed to become even more powerful. For many musicians, it began to feel that they either needed giant promotional funding or ever more inventive distribution strategies.

One such strategy was to accept that recorded music was a loss leader. The received wisdom today amongst huge swathes of the industry is that recorded music is a means to an end rather than an end in itself. You release tracks and albums not because they are a sustainable form of exchange or a stand-alone piece of art, but as a calling card for gigs. Established artists and major labels reacted to the bottom falling out by diversifying their revenue streams, safe in the knowledge that they had options. They could strike licensing deals, make TV shows, release fashion ranges, align themselves with brands, and go on perpetual tour. It's the little guy who really needs recorded music to be worth something. If you sell five thousand copies of your CD, you can just about scrape a living. That gives you independence as a musician. But if we live in a world where recorded music—the culmination of years of creative work—is worthless, then what options for survival and meditative creativity remain? And yet even the penniless independent began to wonder if giving tracks away on social media and via blogs might be the only way to get traction.

So some artists began to give music away for free. Concluding that it was likely to get pirated anyway and that in today's climate, they were unlikely to see any substantial financial returns, many musicians felt that the promotional value of giving music away for free was greater than the return they could expect by trying to sell it. This tactic did see some brief success, but as free downloads grew more prevalent, the social networks took an increasingly jaded view of them and grew weary of "sharing" free music. So, in many ways, it was back to square one—but with yet another subliminal nail in the coffin of recorded music's value.

The subtext to the "free model" of recorded music was an ever-swelling sense of entitlement on the part of the listener. And that is as much a problem for the listener as for the artist. When you feel entitled to something, when you expect something, when you are blasé about something—does it actively limit the depth of your appreciation? The issue isn't just that musicians feel taken for granted or unable to make a basic living from releases—but that listeners have become idle "consumers." "No effort was made in the acquisition of this music" could be a virtual sticker on most digital releases. And it is arguable that emotional outlay as well as its symbolic representation (the parting of hard-earned cash) is an integral part of any experience—especially a lasting one.

With streaming royalties being the stuff of black comedy and SoundCloud somehow managing to cobble together a business model that makes artists and content providers actually pay for the privilege of being listened to, things are unmistakably dire. But perhaps the most insidious idea touted about is that music should be free and public. The emotional blackmail frequently put to artists is that by attempting to monetize, they are somehow desecrating art. It is an argument generally proposed by people who would laugh you out of the workplace if you suggested they toil for the glow of their craft.

There was a time when making music free and divorcing it

from a material price was the most profound statement an artist could make. Indeed, when Jean Michel Jarre made a single copy of *Music for Supermarkets*—a conceptual predecessor to *Once Upon a Time in Shaolin*—he actually encouraged its piracy when it was played on Radio Luxembourg. Except this was a time when piracy was a challenge to corporate interest and the establishment. Today, piracy actively reinforces the establishment by disenfranchising the independent whose sole revenue stream is the music itself.

It could well be said that the most profound statement an artist can make today is to put a price on his music and achieve it. It speaks to sustainability for the artist and their ability to make a living through their art without a second job to subsidize it. And from the listener's perspective, surely part of experiencing music is the knowledge that you are contributing back to the artist—building a circle of human support for something you appreciate. We really aren't talking about faceless corporate entities anymore—the Robin Hood school of music piracy has been wholly subverted by the very forces it once challenged.

But on a deeper level, it forces people who have lost touch with the idea of recorded music as a piece of art to reevaluate their perceptions. And that includes musicians themselves. To strip away the indolence that mass access and content saturation have spawned, and realign the emotional connection with a piece of recorded music both as a listener and as an artist. Ubiquity was once the goal of an artist, but even that apparently obvious ambition is being recalibrated as the actual nature of engagement really starts to matter. Getting heard is more difficult than ever, and yet in many ways it's no longer enough.

The sorry truth about our society is that if something is free or too easy it will eventually become valueless. If something is not done to rein these dynamics back in, we risk losing our respect for and relationship with music on levels far more primal than economics. And yet if one looks at money as a symbolic means of establishing value, and exclusivity as a reflex trigger of desire, then perhaps the reassertion of such frameworks is the only way to stem the digital tide of anonymity, corporate blandness, and surface engagement. Whether this experiment could in any way generate a new depth of connection with music remained to be seen, but we were proud to be asking the question.

So we needed a digital home. Our camel train had wandered the deserts in nomadic style, but now we needed a website and a press release. This project always had to take a different route from any other Clan album; we needed to build in a middleman, a new company whose sole focus was the album. We needed to insulate the rest of the Clan from any backlash and we needed to create a point of contact for anyone who wanted to get involved, from press to buyers, that we alone would be in control of. No labels, no management companies, and no PR firms. Back to motherfucking basics.

We built a website called Scluzay, representing a largely illusory behind-the-scenes company that was managing concept and sale alike. Adorned with atmospheric images and Latin titles that sprinkled a sense of the antique, the website was a brief description of the concept, the album, and then the all-important contact page, with an uncompromising manifesto thrown in for good measure. What with the goal of making millions rather than burning them, we were kind of the anti-KLF, but Bill Drummond and Jimmy Cauty's culture-jamming mischief mainlined through my fractured perspectives. The Justified Ancients of Wu Wu.

The next step was to drop a dime to the press. And this is where things started to get deliciously surreal. In a nutshell . . . they didn't believe a fucking word of it. To this day, we still don't know if they saw the proximity of our contact to April Fool's Day as too much of a coincidence to risk, but many global outlets and cultural leaders weren't having any of it. We had contacted six major media titles, and the only person who didn't just dismiss it out of hand was Zack O'Malley Greenburg at *Forbes*.

There are three ways to launch a story. One is to put out a press release to a mailing list of contacts, from bloggers to the *New York Times,* and let them report it. A second is to line up a day or two of back-to-back interviews with a broad range of press, from bloggers to the *New York Times.* And the third is to go with one exclusive. If it's a good enough story, it will spiral from that ground zero, and you build a trusted relationship with a single journalist. Also, what with our one-copy-exclusive concept, going with a single-outlet exclusive made sixteen shades of sense.

And *Forbes* had the right kind of credentials for us. We didn't want to launch this in the music press, which was too niche; it would be announcing the conceptual limits of our ambition. This was way more than a music story: it was an art story, a society story, an economic story, and a music story all rolled into a gleaming silver box. The first point of launch had to be establishment as fuck in order to set the resonant frequency from the get-go. The first step to smashing current perceptions of music was right here. *Rolling Stone* may have been a more obvious choice. But *Forbes* was a trumpet of intent—a piercing siren in the hood.

The risk was that it would look too much like a financial move, aligning ourselves with a magazine built on the analysis and celebration of wealth. Cynics (like myself) would immediately question the symbolism, but they would be missing the point—the choice of media partner was key to starting a real debate. And when all's said and done, whether the album sold in a deafening clamor or withered on the media vine, the debate was everything. If that didn't take hold, we would have failed.

Zack was understandably very cagey. But while he was guarded to say the least, he was prepared to kick the tires and dig a little deeper. The initial e-mails had been sent out in Cilvaringz's name because you can't have RZA cold-calling journalists, whatever the story. It ain't a strong look. But obviously Cilvaringz's limited profile begged all kinds of questions, so we had always figured that once we had a potential media partner, then and only then could the Abbot be brought in to lay a seal. Sure enough, Zack needed to verify with RZA through multiple channels—his Twitter, his e-mail, the phone—I mean, what was to stop us getting in a talented impersonator to play the role of RZA? Zack was nobody's fool, and the due was extremely diligent.

Still with a nagging sense of disbelief, Zack finally came aboard. Phone calls flew and dates were set for release. The breakdown had been building, the drum rolls hitting a thunderous roar. Wild for the night . . . Let the beat drop.

ZEPHYRUS

March 26, 2014. We were live. The *Forbes* story had been posted. It was a surrender to fate, that moment of release when you've done everything you can and all that's left is to trust the vagaries of a volatile media and the particle accelerator of reflex and response.

There was an eerie digital silence—a lone voice in the neon jungle. Nerves were jangling, fingernails gnawed to the bone. How would it play? Had we managed to present the idea in a solid enough form to survive the inevitable waves of skepticism? Had we done enough?

With Google News on permanent refresh on one tab and the Scluzay e-mail open in another, we downed a few nervous drops of H_2O and twitched a little further. Shit—what if it doesn't take?

And then—just like that—in a split second . . . it went absolutely fucking nuts.

The next few hours felt like jumping aboard the Times Square ticker and barebacking it at breakneck speed through the matrix of global news. Minute by minute the story flashed across the world, as everyone from the *Guardian* to the *Sydney Morning*

Herald chimed into the fray. The inbox began stacking up with requests for comment from some of the most prestigious institutions out there . . . the *New York Times,* the BBC, *Rolling Stone, Time, Billboard,* Bloomberg—some of the very same outlets that had passed on the original story now sprang into action, each looking for an exclusive angle, that element no one else had.

And while it may have been their job to source a new take on a red-hot story, ours was to say as little as possible. Our logic was twofold. First, we wanted the fundamental pillars of the story to resonate without being muddied by tangents. And second, all we really had at this point was an album, an idea, and a day in the spotlight. We still didn't have any answers or "what nexts," and the only way to preserve any real integrity would be to stay relatively quiet and not beat the self-glorifying drum into anesthesia.

Our primary weapon at this stage of the campaign was mystique—and nurturing that had to involve shutting the fuck up and not overexplaining. If our first goal was to provoke a debate, then playing too vocal a role in that debate would skew it irrevocably. So we shut the fuck up and let it roll.

The first beachhead was inevitably the news reporting; we were still a few hours short of the op-ed takes. The press thus far seemed astonishingly receptive to the idea, which mercifully confirmed my instinct that coming from Wu-Tang, this had a very different flavor than, say, if it had come from Kanye. Coming from Kanye, this would have been a story of bling and ego—rightly or wrongly. But the deep soul pressure of the Clan and the performance art dimension that infused the fabled badlands of Shaolin made even those who suspected a gimmick step back and give it a chance.

The first indications of the fog of war began popping up in the inbox within the first hour or two. People asking when it was being released, where they could get a copy, when it was coming out in Asia, and my personal favorite—when will it be on Pirate Bay? Either that last one was coming from a deadpan comedy genius or there was still work to be done getting the point across.

Bursting at the seams by this stage, the inbox was a fascinating tapestry of institutions, the press, heartfelt praise for the project . . . and a torrent of violent abuse. The fans? Well, the fans were very fucking far from impressed. And can you blame them?

From many a fan's perspective, this was treason of the highest order. This junior monk Cilvaringz had been fucking shit up. Suddenly he was Yoko—infiltrating the Clan, weaselling his way into RZA's confidence and pouring poison into his ear. It was like a Staten Island Hamlet—poison in the ear heralding the collapse of a dynasty. And as the reaction grew increasingly bitter, largely in the comment sections of all these articles popping up throughout the Web, it opened up something of a paradox and gave us another insight into our own evolving concept.

Now, if I were a fan, I'd be fuming that the crew I'd supported for twenty years was withholding an album from me, and if I were feeling slighted and cynical, I'd chalk it up to greed instantly. Sold-out motherfuckers—it was betrayal over filthy lucre.

It was clear, and totally understandable, that people hadn't realized the limb we were out on. The album had cost a fortune to make, not least because of the requisite secrecy and the extenuating circumstances of production. So whatever it sold for, creating it had already cost more than twice as much as a normal album, which made for some pretty questionable economics if this was all about profit. And if this didn't fly, it was going to be game over. No option to keep trotting out albums and touring ad infinitum to preserve a stable income. Nope: the Clan would be a laughingstock if this started to unravel, or if it leaked, or if no one wanted it. Shit, this was like going all in on a hand of Texas Hold'em, because everyone felt the debate and the symbolism were worth the fallout.

It raised another question. Who owes whom? Do artists owe the fans for supporting them and making their careers? Or do the fans owe the artists for sharing their music and soundtracking the years? The obvious answer is that it's a mutually supporting cycle, where everyone gets something out of the exchange—capitalism's way of artists being supported by those who love their work. But that social contract had just been torn up and burned on the embers of the old ways.

"You owe us this album." But do they? Have things tipped too far when an artist can't do what he chooses with a piece of music he's created? If we wanted to send the album to the moon, what then? Would that be okay? Wasn't it okay to try and make a bigger statement with this album instead of flinging it back into the swamp of anonymity which so many of today's releases sink into? Well, for many it just flat wasn't. But fuck me; leaving aside the platinum-selling Clan's twenty years at the top of the game, Cilvaringz had put together this six-year magnum opus with his mentor—and only one person might ever hear it. That's heart-wrenching for any artist. He was destined to be the single-copy-album guy, never the "he made that amazing album" guy. There were sacrifices all around.

The opinion pieces were slowly finding their way into the

ether. And it was incredibly heartening to see how seriously the writers were taking the project. There may well have been suspicions about being seen to validate what might turn out to be a marketing stunt, but to their immense credit, most authors engaged with the issues and the ideas rather than taking the judgmental route. Tabloid hysterics and highbrow aloofness were sidestepped and a genuine debate began to take hold. Even the astonishingly few writers who abhorred the idea actually argued the concept and played the ball rather than the man. And that in itself was a beautiful thing.

As we spoke tentatively to a few key media outlets trying to see if it was remotely in the interest of the concept to talk more about it, another phenomenon was playing out in our newly christened Scluzay inbox. A key component of the original *Forbes* story was the promised exhibition phase, and it seemed that art funds and museums had embraced the idea, and were writing in furiously. Now obviously, having got this far, we were thinking the Tate or the MoMA—when you go big, you have to go seriously big, not least because this entire concept was existentially real in the media alone. That's the thing about expectations: Surpass them by a millimeter and you're Caesar. Fall below by a millimeter and you're dumped in an unmarked grave.

That's the fundamental problem with an economic model based on perpetual growth. It doesn't matter if a company makes $2 billion, if they made $2.5 billion the year before, that's failure. The $2 billion profit they just made becomes a footnote to the carousel of excess. So with everything geared to manufacturing desire and keeping the tills ringing artificially high, no wonder resources are being pillaged by short-termism on steroids. What is actually gained and what is actually produced is an irrelevance. Every expectation needs to be beaten, every move needs to be bigger than the last. And if you're going to throw something this dramatic onto the table, you'd better make damn sure you understand that dynamic.

So it was with a heavy heart that we had to say no to so many of the excellent museums and wonderful art funds that wanted to help support the idea. They got it, they wanted to go out on a limb with us, and even if some might say they were in it for the publicity, it didn't feel like that from where we were sitting. Which was the point at which we found ourselves villains of our own piece—judging on appearances rather than substance, but without a hefty shot of realism, this concept would founder where it stood. To all those we didn't work with, a heartfelt apology, but we only had one shot with this and we had to pick and choose which ideals we were prepared to fight for.

Meanwhile, we had some calls in to the Tate. If we could get an exhibition of the album in the Tate Modern, we would have a concrete new step after the launch of the initial story. The Tate was very polite and stalled with a consummate elegance. Cilvaringz had been introduced to senior figures by Vanessa Branson, Richard's sister and a patron of the arts, so they couldn't just tell us to take our vulgar language and gold chains back to whatever gutter we came from without at least pretending to mull it over. It was a rather tender exercise in flimflam and gently perfumed fuck-offs that culminated in the extraordinarily irony-free line

> Any music we have programmed thus far has been
> from a perspective of it being rooted in dialogue with
> art practice, and although I cannot say I have observed
> any direct connections between artists and the

Wu-Tang Clan I think there is an interesting crossover with contemporary art in terms of their political/ collective approach.

Talk about egregiously missing the point. It appeared that art was a walled garden in the eyes of the Tate, and with no direct connection to artists, music wasn't deemed garden-party appropriate.

And then an e-mail dropped in with a Sotheby's suffix. Chap named Benjamin Hanbury-Aggs. Of all the hookah joints in all the world—he was in Marrakech and wanted to talk.

The game was afoot.

MOMENTUM

Perhaps the most intriguing aspect of this project was the sheer scale of the blank canvas before us. There was no template for selling a single copy of an album, no identifiable set of collectors or buyers, no clear medium for the sale, no legal structure whatsoever. The true nature of the *Forbes* story and the ensuing media storm transcended publicity alone—it was the hoisting of a sail. Where the winds would take it was still a wholly unknown quantity, and like the best paradoxes, the dragon was scorching its own tail.

We needed the press to give the album context and a sense of three-dimensional reality (ironically enough for the most physical album ever). You couldn't start a debate, let alone a sale process, without it. And you couldn't start approaching auction houses or brokers with such a bizarre-sounding idea without the concept being made "real" somehow by the media. And what that translated to was that you couldn't presequence any kind of strategy without the story—once it took its own course, it would be a question of surfing the wave that came pulsing out.

There's a concept in Taoism, *wu-wei,* which roughly translates as "swimming with the current." It's often misquoted as "non-action," but it's really about letting the energy and the nature of things flow through you—acting as a conduit for universal rhythm rather than allowing your conscious, linear mind to impose structure that ultimately disrupts rather than enhances.

Now, you may think those are some pretty lofty ideals to be weaving into this tale, halfway between a press story and a business meeting, but take them as you will.

The Sotheby's e-mail felt portentous. Some real omen shit. It wasn't so much that one of the world's most hallowed art companies was in touch—they were always on the map. It was that the guy writing was actually on holiday in Marrakech. What were the chances?

With RZA on the West Coast, we had an eight-hour time difference, so conference calls ran late—and the midnight strategy chats that punctuated the journey were well under way. We had a long discussion about the idea of going with Sotheby's, and knowing that he'd be unreachable for the actual meeting, the three of us needed to analyze the fuck out of the various options. I was gung ho about the idea, feeling that if we could get an established art institution and high-end salesman on board, we could breathe a little easier about the mechanics of the project. Cilvaringz was equally enthusiastic—having a centuries-old institution give its seal to hip-hop culture had huge symbolic strength. And RZA, while seeing both those angles, wanted us to tread carefully and not make any rash decisions. People were reaching out to him through different channels, and with his inbox running hot with major-label executives and enterprising creative agencies, there were some interesting leads to follow—so let's not sign anything quite yet.

Cilvaringz and I strolled into the cozy grace of Grand Café de la Poste, a monument to colonial style and exactly the kind of café Rick would be running if his beautiful friendship with Louie turned sour. We met Ben, whom we instantly felt comfortable with. It was definitely a meeting of worlds, and while his polite formality did raise a twinkle, his warmth and sincerity were unmistakable.

He had felt the significance of his being in Marrakech when the news broke as keenly as we had, and despite his being young and clearly rather junior at the company, we wanted to try and make this work with him. Or at least conduct some heavy reconnaissance together. If there was some way that he could bring this project to his seniors, get a seat at the table for its duration, and reap the rewards of its success, then that would be another tick in the win column. Having discussed the possible trajectories within the Sotheby's ecosystem, we decided that Ben would go back to New York, put some feelers out, and get back to us in the next week or two.

As we left, Cilvaringz glanced at his phone and looked back up with a glint in his eye. Ben Horowitz, billionaire venture capitalist, hip-hop fan, and investor in rap lyric site Genius, had just tweeted that he planned to buy the album. There it was, clear as day: he meant to have it.

So did we need Sotheby's at all? Maybe we should just phone Ben Horowitz and cut out the middleman. But hang on: First off, do we really want to be making serious phone calls off the back of a fucking tweet? And second, even if he was panting at the table with cash-stuffed suitcases, did we really want to conduct the sale in that manner? Yes, it might be quick and commission free, but we needed the album to follow the path of an artwork—it needed to be sold as such and not just be a straight exchange. A quick sale would just be a 1 percent story—where was the art in that?

We had to prioritize finding an art-world partner over finding a buyer. If Ben Horowitz was serious, it would be more elegant all around if he spoke to an art professional rather than us so that the integrity of the concept would remain intact. Art-world partner—that was the mission as it stood. We can say music is art until we're blue in the face, but we live in a world of symbols, tribes, and conventions. To make art, and indeed to make a point, you have to absorb, harness, bend, and break that social architecture.

Meanwhile, the inbox had become the comedic gift that kept on giving. We were starting to receive increasingly random e-mails from hoaxers and nutters alike. The first classic was when Mark Zuckerberg got in touch offering $10 million for the album from his little-known mark.zuckerberg@gmail.com e-mail address. Clearly he was deep undercover, and it was particularly cunning of him to pretend he didn't understand the basic rules of grammar and spelling. Sharp motherfucker, that Zuckerberg—no wonder Harvard couldn't contain him. And then there was a certain Miss Harmsworth, who pledged her virginity for a single listen of the album.

There was a fault line of seriously low-end wind-ups too. "Yo bitches—I'll give you 10 bucks for it" and stuff of that ilk. Just made you wonder who has the time to write such painfully lame shit. I mean, if you're going to mock us, at least do it in style.

Enter Mr. Scaramanga Silk. Now, THIS dude was high end. First off, he refused to pay more than a million dollars for it. Like it: by lowballing, he made the e-mail look that much more serious. Checked the e-mail suffix and it looked like an actual domain rather than another Gmail or Yahoo account. Reading through the e-mail, it did seem fairly legit; he had copyright concerns, leak concerns, all the kind of things that would have actually been playing on the mind of an interested party. And then he told us what he planned to do with it:

> The vinyl shall be transported to the Shaolin Temple, in Henan province, China. From this location, it will be unveiled and displayed to the world. In order to make this a "one-time" event both in terms of where it is situated and as a recording, we will then proceed to use Shaolin Kung Fu to transform the work into microscopic fragments. One million pieces of vinyl shall be created from this exercise. I will then proceed to tour the work and display it around the globe with open debate as to the artistic merit of the act. Gimpo will film all parts of this journey. Each fragmented piece will then be made available to the public at £1 each so that mementos of the legendary work can be owned by the masses. Of course, a collector is welcome to purchase the work in its entirety and can reassemble it if they so wish (but I imagine they may get some snap, crackle and pop on playback). The real debate will then ensue as to whether or not the owner (myself) made a duplicate of the album before the event. Only I will know.

Fucking classic. We had to phone RZA right there and then to tell him—this was right up his street. Some belly laughs and a tip of the hat to Mr. Silk later, some due diligence was in order. There was no evidence of this guy anywhere online apart from a heavily sarcastic letter to a music publication, a website that led nowhere, and a Twitter account that suggested he was an electronic musician. It was obviously a hoax, but damn, it was fun, and if someone had really come along wanting to smash a piece of vinyl into a million pieces in a Shaolin temple and sell them at a buck a pop, we would have loved it on so many levels.

And then something rather unexpected happened. Someone offered $5 million for the album.

We'd never wanted to put a figure on the album. It didn't feel classy, for one thing, but more to the point, a fundamental strand of this experiment was about letting the market decide. The album's financial worth was never going to be decided by what we said it was, but by what someone out there was prepared to pay for it.

This offer checked out. We were at $5 million within a week. With the momentum still riding high, the temptation to cash in and get the fuck out was pretty seductive. Some real snake-in-the-Garden-of-Eden shit. The hype would die down if we went through a lengthy process with someone like Sotheby's, and we'd lose the silly-season impulse of the current landscape. Bottom line, as time went on, it would be more difficult to sell. Five million dollars. Now. You'd have to be made of ice not to melt a little.

There were only two problems. One went back to the need for the project to take the trajectory of an art piece and not be traded in an L.A. conference room. Sell it like this and you have a shitload of cash and one weak-ass statement. And there was another issue. We realized that the concept hadn't fully penetrated through the initial story and resulting analysis. We were selling a sole edition. Not a master copy.

Announcing you have a single-copy album and you're selling it to one collector to reestablish physicality, economic value, and experiential connection to a piece of music is one thing. Announcing that, then letting whoever buys it stick it on iTunes, license it for a film, and press CDs isn't revolutionary: it's the most pompous record deal in history.

It's basically like going to the press, smearing a load of bullshit about art around the place, and then doing a record deal that you've jacked the price on because of the hype. Still, $5 million record deals are pretty rare in this day and age, even with film licensing in the mix. So I guess it was a massive compliment, but there wasn't a shadow of a doubt that the party in question wanted to treat this exactly like any other album. I wondered what Mr. S would have to say about this—opting for conceptual titanium over securing a profitable investment—but he was cool. He wasn't in this for the money, either. And for an investor, that's saying something.

Press requests were bulging every which way to sunrise. We still had a strict moratorium on commenting further, which came as a surprise to everyone, especially the press. It just didn't add up that a hip-hop supergroup had laid down a gauntlet like this and didn't want to take every opportunity to make as much noise about it as possible. Surely we needed an outlet to tell everyone how great we were, how great the album was, how great the concept was, and bank as much free advertising as possible. Except we didn't, because amazingly enough, we weren't full of shit.

Diving back into the Lao-Tzu archive, another Taoist classic:

"He who knows does not speak. He who does not know, speaks." Well, we had the extended mix of that on 45. We'd done our speaking, but without something concrete that elevated or added to the idea, silence was still golden. Except for one thing. RZA had been scheduled to do a heavy round of promotional press for months. Nothing to do with Wu-Tang; it was for his latest film, *Brick Mansions*.

Now, if you've produced a film, the last thing you want is the press round you've spent heavily on to promote your film being hijacked by a totally unrelated story involving one of your stars. RZA didn't want to talk about the album, and the studio sure as hell didn't want RZA talking about it. There was another, tragic layer, too—Paul Walker had died in heartbreaking circumstances and *Brick Mansions* was one of his last films. Which made it even more tawdry to discuss the album.

Being a consummate professional, RZA shut down all discussion of the album despite the fevered interest. As far as anyone was concerned, it was in the hands of the experts—which, ironically and truthfully enough, were ourselves. We were the experts because there was no such field in existence and we'd given more thought to the idea of a single-copy music album than anyone else out there. So experts we were. But there was so much speculation by a charging infantry of bloggers that we finally decided we could perhaps mention the $5 million offer at the end of the *Brick Mansions* press blitz. It was our first verified offer, after all, and it would at least anchor the idea in some kind of real-world metric. Fuck it. We had to give the press something, and at least this was an actual development.

Inevitably enough, though, we were now the $5 million album. It was, in hindsight, a mistake to put that out there, because suddenly the conversation was solely about money again.

The irony was that this project was both about the money and not about the money. To make the point about value and the need for recorded music to be worth something, it had to sell for a lot of money. The price tag was part of the statement—it literally had to be worth a fortune to comment on the psychology of the unattainable versus that of the ubiquitous. If tangible value is measured in money units, and people aren't prepared to pay small amounts of those money units for something, what happens when you deny access and make it a one-off exclusive? What value do we put on it then? And furthermore, we couldn't give all the profits to charity, either. We could give some, even most, of the profits away, but by fuck we did have to keep a share, because part of the point was that artists should get paid and when they sell a CD they should be able to live off the proceeds in some way. It wasn't about delighting in the money per se—but money needed to be involved at every step to make the point about value. Another paradox. I did love this project.

ESTABLISHMENT

A week or so later, with his North African tan fading in the shadow of Manhattan steel, Ben gave us a status update from Sotheby's. Rather unsurprisingly, there were some hefty differences of opinion within the organization about the wisdom of their association. It didn't take an expert in seventeenth-century miniatures to figure out their dilemma.

On the one hand, Sotheby's didn't acquire its grande dame status by hightailing after every bandwagon that rolled past. Reputation was key in the art game, and the reward of all the publicity that would go with selling this album was overshadowed by the horror some of their distinguished clientele would register at their involvement with anything as vulgar as a hip-hop album. It felt flimsy to them, they didn't fully understand the idea, they couldn't trust us not to embarrass them, they didn't know who to pitch it to, and somewhere deep down they thought this album had about as much cultural validity as a diamond-encrusted thong once worn by Beyoncé.

And yet, if they did sell it, they would gain some of the contemporary relevance all hallowed institutions seek when their shareholders are ready to strip the mahogany fittings at the first sniff of a slowdown. They needed to keep their hand in with new ideas and new generations to keep fresh blood flowing in, and if they could sell this, it would add a positive string to their bow and place them on the cutting edge of the arts while remaining custodians of its commodified history.

Ben, who had actually met us and felt we were people Sotheby's could do business with, was pushing for conversations at executive level. It seemed that the only department that could realistically take this on was Special Projects, headed up by a certain Mr. David Redden. And he was currently consumed by the sale of a $45 million Stradivarius viola.

We did our research on Mr. Redden, and he certainly did have an impressive repertoire of bonkers sales under his belt—from an original copy of the Magna Carta to a dinosaur skeleton. It looked great on paper, and it didn't do our egos any harm at all to picture the album sold at a Sotheby's auction alongside seminal documents and primal history.

Still, it was hard to reconcile David Redden with this project. We had no doubt whatsoever of his pedigree, talent, and experience, but to judge by videos we'd seen of him wielding a gavel, there wasn't a whiter man in existence. It was very clear to us that he could only speak to a limited world. And there was nothing wrong with that: it was his world and they probably loved him just the way he was. But this project?

There was another factor—how about our fucking reputation? It was one thing seeing a Wu-Tang album sold at Sotheby's, but entirely another aligning it with someone so fundamentally establishment that it would feel like we'd gone begging to the white guys in suits for approval.

You could smell generational friction in the air and a sense of frustration in those pushing for Sotheby's to take the deal. Ben was exceptionally discreet, and you could tell at times he was gently stalling us, but we just knew how it was playing. Redden wasn't keen, others at executive level were, so rather than refuse outright, he made us an offer. Start the bidding at $500,000— not a penny more—and place it in a music memorabilia auction. A music fucking memorabilia auction. Talk about the antithesis of the whole concept.

Being lined up alongside Bob Dylan's Y-fronts and Elvis's last burger was frankly a bigger insult than being told to take our album and shove it up our Queens Boulevards. As if we needed any help selling music as fucking music. This had to be in a contemporary art auction, or what was the point? This album was contemporary art. If you don't get that, then we have nothing left to discuss. Though we didn't phrase it quite so heroically. Options were still key. So we "took it under advisement."

The very next morning an e-mail dropped in from a fellow named Gabriel Butu, from a company called Paddle8. I had vaguely heard of Paddle8, and from what I knew, it was a young start-up trying to drag the art market into the twenty-first century. With a little more research, we had a pretty good handle on their emerging business model. The idea was to hold rolling online auctions and aim for the midmarket, trading largely in the $50,000–$100,000 range, looking at volume over high-value single items, slashing costs by eschewing an extensive physical operation, and basically being an auction house for the Uber age.

Their investor list was impressive, which certainly suggested that they would go far; the company felt fresh, young, and funky, but there were two nagging issues. First, what a bizarre irony to sell the world's most physical album through the world's most digital auction house. And second, could they actually sell the damn thing for millions?

RZA, Cilvaringz, and I agreed that I'd take the call; we didn't want either of them on the line at this stage. Paddle8 was pitching us, and you don't put your main players in the room to receive a preliminary inquiry. So Gabriel and I had a chat, and despite our interest having been piqued on paper, I came away from the call without a great deal of hope. It was evident that Gabriel's job on the call was to sell me on Paddle8 in its most blueprinted form and put the album up for online auction. We were never going to do that; it had nowhere near enough drama for something on this scale, and when I angled for maneuver, he simply wasn't authorized to flex.

So Sotheby's was "under advisement" and Paddle8 wasn't looking good. Had to be Christie's.

We hadn't wanted to contact Christie's while we felt there was still traction with Sotheby's. Every other motherfucker played them off against each other to squeeze the best deal, but we weren't any other motherfucker. We were outsiders who needed to establish trust and honor, to get past the instinctive panic ringing through any conservative institution as they went into business with the Wu-Tang Clan.

We had been flicking through the list of Christie's department heads, wondering which one to approach. Our thinking went beyond categories like music, popular culture, and contemporary art and took in factors like age and appearance, thanks to the Redden episode. Judging books by their covers again—but fuck it, stereotypes do often pan out.

It was at that point that a *Billboard* article entitled "Why Wu-

Tang's Stunt Might Actually Work" hit the silver streams of cy-
berspace with a quote from someone at Christie's named Caitlin
Graham. It read:

> This is an exciting concept that could resonate well
> with devoted collectors of pop culture. An auction is
> an interesting way to sell something like this, since
> you can open up the bidding on a global level and let
> the market decide how high the price will go.

Okay, so the upside was that they were making positive noises
in the press. The downside: "pop culture" felt like code for music
memorabilia. Not an auction alongside Warhol paintings.

Cilvaringz cut straight to the heart of the matter: "Let's just
write directly to the CEO."

I had my doubts. You didn't just write to CEOs over things
like this. Still, what did we have to lose? Steven Murphy's e-mail
was conveniently online, so fuck it—we dropped him a line. And
to his huge credit, he forwarded it on to a senior executive named
Cathy Elkies who was keen to have a conversation. We were impressed. This felt more dynamic and plugged in than Sotheby's
already.

But we didn't want to enter negotiations with no leverage—
and the Sotheby's offer was only leverage on paper. We weren't
sure we could sound convincing about wanting to take it, so we
decided to have a final look at Paddle8.

The CEO was a chap named Alexander Gilkes. Google was
generous with its results, and there were several factors that
leapt out of the research phase. He was a darling of the society
pages, dashingly good looking, devilishly charming, effortlessly

debonair, and connected to the elites in a way that seemed to outstrip the company itself. The company might be small, but with him at the helm, you wouldn't bet against them growing into a major player. Poring through interviews, it was also mercifully apparent that he wasn't a dick. I've never trusted society pages—in fact, I have a deep-rooted suspicion of them—but he seemed neither vacant nor arrogant, but really rather fun.

We had also been at Eton together. I had departed under a torrential cloud after two years when differences of opinion over behavioral standards had blossomed into a rather underwhelming expulsion. Alexander had been younger than me, and I hadn't known him at school, but I decided that however tenuous the connection was, it was worth throwing into an e-mail to get him onto the next, and potentially final, call.

What followed was just the kind of quality episode we wanted to see more of with this project. From the sublime to the ridiculous.

Cilvaringz and I took the call with Gabriel and Alexander on the other end. Alexander swept into the video conference slightly late, slightly out of breath, and only slightly briefed. Settling in, the first words out of his mouth were "Will R.Z.A. be joining us?" It was a slight alarm bell hearing the letters spelled out like that, but nothing compared to the glorious moment when he asked whether Dirty Old Bastard was on the album.

Ol' Dirty Bastard was a legend no matter how you cut it. He was a radiant spirit—in heart, soul, and the freewheeling symphony of life. One of the magic ones, he died at thirty-six. Laid to rest in the 36th Chamber and forever shining, he was the Clan's tragedy, the Shakespearean moment of mortality that both tore the fabric and gilded it.

Dirty Old Bastard, on the other hand, sounded like a guy in a raincoat flashing women in a parking lot. I saw Cilvaringz visibly stiffen. You could see what he was thinking: Fuck, it's a young David Redden. It was an early left hook. But we pressed on.

"Look, Alexander. Cutting to the chase, we like the look of your company and we can definitely see the merits in partnering with a young, hungry up-and-comer. But we aren't putting this in an online auction."

"Okay, fine."

"Say we wanted to do an individual auction for this; say we wanted it to take place at some completely unconventional venue and feature only this one lot—we could make it a signature event with performances, screenings, an exhibition, and an auction to climax on. How would you feel about that?"

"Sounds like a cracking idea."

"Or maybe a private sale."

"Absolutely."

This guy just kept saying yes to everything. And not in a bullshit way, either. This was someone we could really work with. We loved his energy. Cilvaringz even forgave him the Dirty Old Bastard line. This was one charming motherfucker. And he had a twinkle in his eye. The all-important twinkle.

The school thing cropped up at the end of the call in a fumbled grope of awkward flirting. I almost regretted bringing it up in advance of the call as the conversation had gone so smoothly on a business level that it seemed a shame to try and manufacture a personal connection. He'd heard of me, too. Apparently I'd been notorious. Fuck—what had he heard? Was this going to prove counterproductive? I'd made a fair few enemies, largely by being a bit of a dick.

But from that moment on, I was in Paddle8's corner for this deal. RZA and Cilvaringz were nowhere near as convinced as me; they were leaning way more toward Christie's. The whole expectations thing was rearing its head again. The Wu puts *Once Upon a Time in Shaolin* up for auction through Christie's. That's meeting expectations. The Wu go with a relative unknown called Paddle8? Well, no one else must have wanted to touch it. You just knew that without some serious finesse, that's how it would play.

I put down the phone and checked the inbox. A Nigerian tycoon was offering $7 million worth of livestock for the album. And wait, hang on—what's this?

Well, fuck me with a quadrangle. Harvard wanted to debate the album.

OPTIONS

It all comes back to symbols. Maybe it shouldn't have to, maybe true art is the creation of new symbols, but we were trying to shoot existing perceptions through angled prisms. We needed to land somewhere between a mirror and a portal, and what stronger symbol was there in America for the history of ideas than Harvard University.

A postgrad student named Paul Fargues had gotten in touch with us. He wanted to arrange an exhibition of the box, soundtracked by at least some of the music, and hold a discussion of the themes raised by the album. Supported by a high-profile professor, the debate segment had real potential to open new threads and sow new seeds. They were talking about bringing experts from the art world, musicians who'd tried different revenue models, historians, economists, sociologists, and cultural analysts together—throw in a psychologist and we'd have something with real gravity.

All of which begged the question, what were we doing about this listening tour we'd promised in the press? Of all the elements of the concept, that was the one that was rapidly becoming a millstone around our necks. It sounded great in the magisterial sweep of ideal big picture—this swelling wave of excitement engulfing the globe as die-hard hip-hop brothers, aesthetes, and the perennially curious alike flocked to listen in museums and galleries. Recorded music as spectacle, as experience, as monument.

Only thing was, we weren't in a fluffy fictional world of handy narrative arcs. The flaws in the exhibition plan were manifold. For starters, if one of the goals was to sell the album and one of the selling points was exclusivity, then to what degree were we siphoning financial value out of the project by letting the music be played? To what degree were we surrendering core elements of the project? A rather smug devil's advocate would counter by suggesting that if the music was good enough, we would have nothing to worry about; the more people who placed experiential value on it by listening, the more its intrinsic value—artistic and economic—would be enhanced.

Yeah, right—in that fluffy fucking fictional world, maybe. The very nature of the disposable, oversaturated culture of fingertip wow that had driven many of the project's touchstones almost inevitably condemned that logic. Mystique is a profoundly powerful veil—a psychic aphrodisiac whispering a siren call—that delicate brush of silk. Mystique fed more into lust and the masochistic allure of unrequited longing than love itself, but if the collective consciousness of a society is growing increasingly addicted to the dopamine hits of the quickening, part of its therapy had to delay gratification and reconstruct the courtship phase. Can't just keep fucking on the first date—at some point we all need to be romanced. But we were now considering a chastity belt until marriage.

And, well, soaring rhetoric aside, we didn't want the damn thing to leak, either. It was a red rag to a bull, wasn't it? The second we put this album out of reach, every single enterprising, switched-on, disgruntled, innovative motherfucker would be trying to find a way to record it. We went through various scenarios; headphones, airport-style security, transmitter and bug sweeps: you name it, we thought of it. But someone, somewhere, was going to break the firewall. Someone was going to have a mic on a pinhead.

Back in the cuddly mirage of Happytown, a leak shouldn't affect the issues raised by the project, but in the real world, it would be game over. The narrative would distill down to "they tried to stop us having it—we showed them." The leaker would be Robin fucking Hood and we would be pilloried as elitist, pompous, and, worst of all, incompetent.

But one or two really select venues with a heavyweight security operation could work. And bottom line, we knew we had to play some of the music to someone sometime. Every courtship needs to flash a little thigh. We made encouraging noises to Harvard and awaited the next development.

Meanwhile, we were due a powwow with Christie's. Cathy Elkies was lovely; we took to her immediately. And she was joined on the call by Karen Gray, senior legal counsel. What legal issues could there possibly be at this stage?

We swiftly arrived at the conclusion that Karen's role was to protect the company against anything that might bite them in the ass. She was the gatekeeper. She was there to feel us out and hammer as many holes in the project as possible. To this day I'm sure it was meant constructively; she was very engaging and very reasonable, and I believe that she felt that if the idea was still standing after she'd thrown her full arsenal against it, then and only then could it be pursued.

It was actually a huge compliment that demonstrated just how seriously they were taking it. Wave after wave of conceptual, practical, and ethical assaults came flying over the bows, immaculately tailored and artfully presented. There wasn't a foundation left unscathed or a charge left undetonated, and short of entering the real nitty-gritty like legal protections, she fought a mighty fine battle. To this day, we have nothing but the utmost respect for the way Christie's went about things—Karen doing every structural test in the book and Cathy focusing on the potential strategies for sale.

What Christie's were ultimately looking for was cultural validation from as many respected establishment bodies as possible. They weren't buying what we were selling on our word alone, and clearly didn't give a flying fuck about how long our column inches were—and in many ways, good on them. Harvard proved to be a great counteroffensive. Everyone perked up at that, because that was the kind of watermark Christie's needed to feel safe entering the chambers.

It made sense as a strategy for them. They didn't need to go hurtling out on any limbs, they had very little to prove, and while this would be a trophy in an overflowing cabinet if all went well, the backlash if it didn't wouldn't be pretty. They would look naïve and bungling if this all fell apart—and quite frankly, who needs that level of risk in their lives when business is good?

Remember that devil's advocate from a couple of pages back? Turns out he works at Christie's. After several calls, we got down to brass tacks. They were happy to mediate a private sale with extremely limited liability, but if we wanted all the bells and whistles, there were some hoops we'd have to jump through.

They had settled on that narrative of taking it on an exhibition tour. This was naturally presented to us in the most "we're on your side" light as possible—it would create a "halo effect" around the album with each gallery validating it, and if we chalked up enough gold stars, they'd let us play. What they didn't mention is that such a tour would also represent the physical manifestation of the tire kicking Karen had done. If this thing was still standing after a tour of eight to ten galleries, then they would feel safe enough to jump publicly aboard, confident their risk had been minimized.

Couple of issues there: We knew we weren't the Mona Fucking Lisa. We were talking about a living group trying something new with a queue round the block baying for blood and failure. We couldn't risk it for the reasons we'd already considered. But lovely though Karen and Cathy were, we weren't going to go through some fucking brownie point acquisition process. The subtext to the whole conversation was that even though they'd do a private sale as we stood, they didn't fully believe in our concept. They'd be our broker, but they were going to ruin the wedding night with the tone of their prenup. Still, it was an option.

Gabriel from Paddle8 was proving to be a total star. We'd had some very constructive chats since the call with Alexander and certainly since the first rather frigid call he and I had shared. He was running the day-to-day on this, and in much the same spirit as Christie's, he wanted to know if there were any bodies and where they were buried. Though he was gentler than Christie's and used a lot more lube.

And this was the thing. Having seen the kind of reservations held by Sotheby's and Christie's, you had to ask yourself, didn't Paddle8 have even more to lose? Christie's and Sotheby's might fall victim to some sniggering, but the bullet would bounce in the long run. With Paddle8, the bullet could be fatal. I mean, maybe we were planning on putting the whole damn thing online once we'd sold it—double-crossing the buyer and delighting the fans. Where would our art-world partner be then? In deep fucking shit, that's where—especially without the protection of reputation and scale.

The split was as pronounced in the Paddle8 offices as anywhere else. Sure this would be a trophy in a newly built cabinet if all went well, but with so many iconoclastic elements to their business model already, wouldn't they be better off trying to convince the industry that they were a safe pair of hands? Not the type of firm that goes galloping after mirages?

They had more to gain and more to lose than anyone else, which already drew them closer to our position. I had wondered throughout the process how the internal decision was made at Paddle8 to green-light their involvement, and on the day it finally sold, head of communications Sarah Goulet told us the story. The executives had met to take a final vote on whether to proceed or not and the count was split down the middle. The offices were getting a face-lift that day, and a guy could be seen hanging a new painting through the glass walls of the conference room. With the painting mounted, he stepped back, checked the angles, and turned around. He was wearing a Wu-Tang T-shirt.

I would have loved them even more then if I'd known that. They were 50-50 on a well-thought-through risk/reward analysis, but unlike Christie's, which wanted to stay in the shallow end with a wet suit, oxygen tank, whistle, and rescue trawler, Paddle8 opened themselves up to a sign from the universe—a moment of pure synchronicity. These guys had soul, and we didn't just want a broker, anyway. We wanted a partner.

And then of course there was the small matter of the number 8. The Wu-Tang Clan have always channeled the rhythms of mathematical harmony—harnessing the patterns, symmetries, and arcane mysticism of numerology. And the thing about symbols is that by infusing them with power, they become real. You can argue whether a certain number has any objective significance—whether its matrix is any more potent than another. But if your consciousness views it as an axis, as a rune, and as a conduit for its vibrational flows, then that number will keep recurring in your reality and slowly take on the silent footprint of magic.

The number 8 entered the equation with the *Wu-Tang Forever* album. Turn a number 8 on its side and you have the infinity symbol. *8 Diagrams* was another album that followed. There are sixty-four squares on a chessboard—eight by eight, with chess being a meditative outlet for the Abbot and long a part of the Wu-Tang landscape. The *Forbes* story was launched on the twenty-sixth of March—2+6. And now we were talking to a company that had the number 8 in its name. It was the echo of the T-shirt epiphany playing out at Paddle8 HQ. This was our sign from the universe.

DIVERSIFYING OUR BONDS

We were starting to see the concept mature in the press. The headline phase had calmed, but articles by copyright lawyers, academics, business commentators, and industry insiders were springing up and adding new layers to the debate. With greater scrutiny came more perspectives, more insights, and more ways of framing the questions the album was asking. It was something of a hydra—every time you cut off one of its heads, two more grew back, and that was just the way we wanted it. The best questions have no right answer, no linear sequence of logic or moral clarity, but dance forever in shifting shades of gray.

Zack from *Forbes* had been pressing to do a follow-up piece that would involve traveling to Morocco and taking a firsthand look at both case and music. I wasn't convinced that we needed to do any more, let alone cooperate in an online documentary whose primary raison d'être was to take a bite from the forbidden sonic fruit, but I was cheerfully voted down. There were two distinct camps throughout the journey, one that felt none of the music should be played at all, and another that wanted to drop tasters. And the interesting thing was, the members of those respective camps kept swapping as circumstances morphed and strategies evolved.

One major thread was the seven-figure offer we had received from a corporation that would allow it to give a single song away. This was seductive on a material level, but there were also arguments that saw the wisdom in such a move. First off, it would mollify a furious fan base to at least a degree—one song free to soften the blow of losing an album. If successful, it could only ratchet up anticipation about the rest of it, confirm that there was real music on this album and that it was fucking dope. And yet the idea of partnering with a corporation filled me with abject horror.

To paraphrase Jane Austen, "it is a truth universally acknowledged that an artist in possession of an album must be in want of a corporate tie-in." The reflex reaction to the standalone economics of recorded music plunging into meltdown was to seek some other means of payment, some other paymaster than the public to keep recorded music from becoming a loss leader for tours, licensing, and merchandise alone. In the vanguard was Jay Z, whose groundbreaking deal with Samsung saw him get paid and keep fans happy by gifting them the music via Samsung hardware. At least, it was a gift if you were buying Samsung hardware.

Jay received huge praise for this innovative business model, but you couldn't help feeling rather empty about it. Well, I couldn't, anyway. I just felt that corporations sterilized everything in their wake, subsuming integrity in shiny plastic and numbing all they touched into a parade of pickpocketing confetti.

Just putting a company name next to what we were doing—any

company, no matter how "cool" its brand management was—would, for me, utterly pillage the conceptual sanctum. However pissed off anyone was about what we were doing and however admiring others were, the fact remained that it was a twenty-first-century anomaly. No corporations were involved. This was between artists, their trusted team, and the world. It was a direct conversation with no PR firms, no corporations, no intermediaries, and no yawningly predictable tricks up its sleeve.

That was the irony about these flashy corporate deals. However inventive the stunt, however creative the angle, partnering with a brand really is about the most conventional move anyone can make these days.

You can shout me down and say that major labels are corporations and that there's no difference between a label logo and a Samsung logo, but while that might stack logically, the two really aren't the same. Not symbolically, anyway. But then, Times Square billboards are perhaps the most accurate symbol for the world we live in—so what the fuck do I know. Enough to value a different set of symbols, I guess.

In the end, we said no to the offer to release a single track. This was too precious to be sullied by conventional associations. But should we just drop one for free with no payday, no brand involvement—just give a single away? It was tempting, but in the end we decided against it. It muddied the waters and confused the messaging. There was barely enough clarity about what we were doing anyway let alone introducing free giveaways. And anyway—what are you saying when you rail against the loss of value in music, make a single copy of an album that's on the market for millions, then give away a single whether you get paid by someone else or not. It's still free to the consumer. Talk about a concept self-destructing if the first tangible aspect of the "let's restore value to music" album is a free single.

But the musical nature of the album needed some kind of window. Sultry mystique is all well and good, but this was tantamount to bringing it out in a burka. The album was a testament to the classic Wu sound, a journey back into the chambers, through raw, jagged beats and dark, stripped-back, liquid funk. But saying that in words only goes so far. Could we, should we, crack open the box ever so slightly? What would Pandora advise?

The tentative answer was yes. But literally a fraction. And not in any kind of substantive quality—just a fleeting moment of eye contact before vanishing back behind closed doors. We decided to go for it via the *Forbes* documentary. Fifty-two seconds of music recorded by a mic in the studio rather than the crystal clarity of a line signal. And they could come see the casing in its palatial residence firsthand. Fuck it—let's roll.

RZA was way too tied up to come to Morocco, and at this stage, we didn't want to bring anything stateside. There was a poetry to where it was; the most secure art-storage facility in New York can't hold a scented candle to the ancient mysteries of the Red City, and Marrakech was an integral part of the story. Snowcapped peaks, arid plains, and medieval walls that nomadic caravans had crossed deserts to behold—a fragment of this album's soul would always remain buried in the ocher soils of Marrakech. It had to be here, and the album had a private palace in the Royal Mansour hotel to call its own. No bar codes, no numbers, no shelving, no scars of modernity, just dignity, majesty, and the scent of orange blossom lingering in the air.

Cilvaringz wanted to delay until RZA was free and could fly

over, but the Abbot was proud to let Cilvaringz step to the public fore and claim his due. So we gave the go-ahead to *Forbes,* and Zack flew over with a cameraman. Cilvaringz had picked a killer verse with Ghostface going in all guns blazing and a soaring note from Cher to crescendo on. There were two fundamental elements to the clip. Ghost sounding heavy as fuck. And Cher guesting on the album.

The press was all over the Cher angle. When we launched the original website, Cilvaringz had credited the pseudonym she used on her very first solo recording, Bonnie Jo Mason, as a guest artist. We figured that what with it being a Google search away, and as one of the few credited guest artists, someone somewhere would have made the connection before now, especially as it had been sitting in plain sight for weeks. *Rolling Stone* had actually left her name out of the original article it ran, which raised the question of why nobody there did a three-second Google search. I mean, if Bonnie Jo Mason was a total nobody, why would she be one of three mentioned guest artists? But then no one else picked up on it, either.

Which is why we all enjoyed a good chuckle when the press went nuts over the "reveal." Cher had been a total star and incredibly cool throughout the process, and this was no different; she sent up a joyous tweet to confirm, before the press turned itself inside out trying to imagine what a collaboration might sound like.

But meanwhile, away from the headlines, the connoisseurs were paying attention. Those beats, Ghost's vibe, that feel, that menacing swagger. Sheeeeeeeeeeet. If those fifty-two seconds were anything to go by, this album was seriously fierce. Christie's could try and get this validated by the fucking pope, but it was being validated as we spoke—by people who actually knew their shit. And they weren't happy. Has liking a piece of music ever generated such a frustrated, angry reaction?

Interview requests were tumbling in like a drunken rugby team. And we decided to go with two of them in London. One was Bloomberg TV, which had promised a sensible discussion with Cilvaringz. We wanted to keep them sweet anyway, as *Forbes,* our main outlet, was a major competitor in the business press, and we didn't want any bad blood. And the other was a BBC radio show, *The Today Programme.*

Now, when I say radio, I'm not talking no Breakfast Club. Or music. Or anything targeted at the youth. No, *Today* is a uniquely British phenomenon and the BBC's flagship current affairs program—an extraordinary achievement at a broadcaster with such televisual reach. Prime ministers and presidents alike come for their grilling as *Today,* with its seven million listeners in a country of seventy million, sets the political and news agendas for the day. That figure as a ratio of population is around what the sitcom *Friends* was pulling in across the U.S. at its peak. And this was a radio news show.

A serious, respected, and quite brilliant institution, this wasn't the kind of frequency that recycled press releases, like so much of the media, nor was it the kind of voice that explored issues unless they had real social, political, economic, or cultural relevance. If there was a dream venue for me to see the album discussed, it was *Today.* RZA and Cilvaringz had never heard of it, of course; it was a very British game of cricket. But they were happy to go with my instinct, even if they did probably wonder why the fuck I was coming across as such a teenybopping fan over a goddamn radio news program.

Both slots went well and did what we wanted them to do—get away from tabloid bullet points and into a deeper discussion of the issues. So the fifty-two seconds were out there and causing a ruckus. Cher's involvement had added another shade to the mystery. We'd made it to my favorite news program. We hadn't looked directly at the corporate Medusa. And we were close to a deal with Paddle8.

Everything was working like clockwork—a quantum clockwork rather than a Newtonian clockwork, but this was the new physics of music. A post-relativity horizon where the electrons were flying across the spectrum and you couldn't predict where the cosmic chips would fall. The fractals of chaos theory undulated around us. There was only one nagging question. What the fuck were we going to do if this album didn't sell?

Only a fool wouldn't keep that eventuality in the forefront of their thinking. The reality was that it was a huge gamble; we had no idea if anyone out there would pay millions for an album. It was an unproven investment. Who knew if the buyer could resell it for the kind of money they outlaid, and they wouldn't be able to commercialize it. It was one thing to build a pair of wings and jump off a cliff, entirely another not to have a safety net somewhere in the ravine.

We needed a cutoff point, too. We needed to set either an auction date or a limited period of availability to finalize a private sale. We couldn't just let this drift indefinitely. And if it didn't sell, we couldn't just come and say, hey, guys, we tried something, it didn't work, it was a worthwhile experiment, let's move on. The world doesn't really work like that; we'd be howled down in the binary language of success or failure. And philosophical inquiry aside, the investor needed his money back.

The obvious move if it didn't sell would be to shrug, then put it out on general release. Except we couldn't do that. You simply can't tell people they are never getting their hands on something despite years of support and loyalty, then come back to them a while later saying actually, guys, you can buy this now because our other plan didn't work out. It's like taking the nice girl to the prom, ditching her for a flirtatious cheerleader, getting ditched yourself for the quarterback, then going back to the girl you abandoned and hoping she still wanted to dance. If she had an ounce of self-respect, she'd tell you to go fuck yourself.

We needed some fail-safes, some options, and some backup plans.

We needed to diversify our bonds.

FLORENCE

The terra-cotta tiles of Brunelleschi's dome sparkled in the sunshine. Nestled into the Tuscan hills, that glorious jewel of contradiction bathed in the soft warmth of an azure sky. The yin and yang of capitalism and culture, intrigue and illumination, violence and the visionary were frescoed into the bedrock.

There really wasn't a more fitting place on earth for a summit. As inspiration alone, meeting to discuss our contribution to the philosophy of art in the birthplace of the Renaissance was a seminal moment, but Florence spoke to so many deeper elements within the nexus.

The Renaissance is often perceived as a movement within the visual arts, but it was the alliance between mercantilism and art that proved its lasting legacy. The Medici Bank was founded in 1397, and within those coffers lay the roots of both the Florentine Renaissance and a disturbingly accurate mirror for our times. As the bank ran flush with cash and branches sprang up across Europe, Medici influence skyrocketed within the Tuscan heartland. In less than forty years, the Medici were the de facto rulers of Florence. Bankers as unofficial kings—ringing any bells? If only the weather was as good on Wall Street.

There were monumental developments within the style and technique of art that coincided with Medici patronage, and like every historical milestone, it was a perfect storm of elements that fused together into a quantum leap. The classical take on the human form, the discovery of perspective to create the illusion of depth, all these advances may have had some kind of impact, but without the rivers of gold flowing under the Ponte Vecchio, we would never have seen such an extraordinary flowering. Cash on its own was utterly sterile—had those currents of artistic change not encountered merchant money, Florence would have doubtless been beautified, but in the fraying robes of the medieval rather than the sumptuous new silks. It was the union of capitalism and art. Money generated beauty, contemplation, transcendence, and communion with our deeper selves—not because you can buy or sell feeling, but because artists had the financial freedom to create as they saw fit. Art was no longer the preserve of the church and had begun to develop a whole new economic model. The lessons of the Florentine Renaissance couldn't be learned through the art alone; the environment in which that art could be created and recognized was just as crucial a catalyst. Economics and experience—the central themes of our concept were the twin pillars the Renaissance was built on.

Now, don't get me wrong—I'm not suggesting a dystopian reality where Goldman Sachs rules the arts, but as a vivid, uncomfortable symbol of the relationship between creation and the economic ability to dream, Florence under the Medici was bang on. And anyway, who do you think is buying art today—the Dalai Lama?

We had evolved to a place in the twentieth century where music could be supported by the public rather than a naked oligarchy and individuals had a vote on which artists would break through. Yet here we stood in the twenty-first century, with patronage by huge corporations superseding the democratic—an endless stream of subsidized crap aimed at twelve-year-olds. All the while, the independents today were being burned by the pirates in a modern-day echo of Savonarola, the Florentine priest who sabotaged his own revolution through puritanical self-righteousness.

I had flown in from London, Cilvaringz from Marrakech, and RZA from Los Angeles. We needed to meet and discuss the full range of issues, from confirming Paddle8 as our partner, to the other Wu-Tang album in the pipeline, to our safety nets if the album didn't sell or the offers were too low. Cilvaringz had e-mailed us the week before to let us know he had a plan to put to the board for what we could do in such an eventuality, and despite our pressing him for details by phone, his innate sense of theater made him hold fire until we were gazing over a magisterial vista. He'd been nursing it since the very start, it would seem.

We were on the terrace at La Loggia in the Piazzale Michelangelo, perched on a hilltop overlooking Florence. Below us was the grand panorama of history, a lagoon of rolling rooftops and glistening marble lapping at the hills as a profound connection to the textures of history anchored in our minds. RZA had chosen the spot, and damn had he nailed it. Fuck boardrooms with commanding views of Central Park—this was the shit.

It was the first time I'd met RZA in person. It's always a

strange one when you've been speaking to someone on the phone for months and swapping regular e-mails. When you finally meet, there's this moment of disconnect between knowing them on a conversational level and their physical reality. And that's only magnified when that individual has a legendary public persona. You kind of forget their public perception, even as you factor it into your strategizing, but it doesn't feel all that real, especially if their field was never your area of expertise. It's an interesting twist.

And after some tentative small talk, we slipped into a groove. RZA had an aura about him, a warmth and a Zen happiness. He seemed totally at ease with himself and I instantly tipped my hat to his interplay of poetic soul and urban intuition. It was all rather surreal sitting there under a Tuscan canopy, plotting a chapter in musical history with one of hip-hop's great statesmen.

First things first: Paddle8. We were a go. It just clicked on so many levels and to write a new, somewhat renegade chapter in the history of art and music alike, only they had the vision and the balls to see it through.

Next up: *A Better Tomorrow,* the new public album from the Wu-Tang Clan. Now this was an interesting intertwining of strands. *Once Upon a Time in Shaolin* had taken so fucking long to make and had been obliged to protect its neck in so many myriad ways through its recording, mixing, and mastering that RZA had never factored it into the scheduling. It could have been ready in 2013, 2014, or 2015 so timing the release date of this new album around *Once Upon a Time* was neither practical nor desirable.

The press had been full of stories about RZA and Raekwon's beef—how Rae wasn't going to do *A Better Tomorrow* and how the album was on indefinite hold. None of which was any of my business; my place in the lives of the Wu began and ended with this one album. To this day, I have neither met nor formed an opinion about any other members of the Clan, and I very much doubt they know who the fuck I am. They were the artists and I was a kind of ideas advisor/business consultant who came on board once the artwork was sealed and delivered. I didn't want to get into any discussions about the internal politics of the Clan—it just wasn't my place.

Still, I'd have been a moron not to be curious. When push came to shove, the disharmony I kept reading about in the press wasn't doing us any favors with *Once Upon a Time,* but it wasn't my question to ask. So I was mighty relieved when RZA volunteered the latest developments, though he remained honorably careful not to discuss any personal or business matters between Clan members.

It seemed that *A Better Tomorrow* was back on track and looking at a November 2014 release date. It was now June, and we all understood the mutually assured damage that would be wreaked by having two irons in the media fire simultaneously. *Once Upon a Time* was a longer game, and even if we signed contracts with Paddle8 tomorrow, it would be a while before they could create a catalog for the piece, assemble some leads, and organize some kind of exhibition to launch the sale phase. We were still at the development stage, and it made sense to delay any more public activity around *Once Upon a Time* until the new year, clearing the way entirely for *A Better Tomorrow* to breathe.

But there was a twist. If *A Better Tomorrow* was the public album and *Once Upon a Time* a law unto itself, then how could at least some of the themes raised by our project be translated to mass production? RZA had a plan up his sleeve, and while he'd alluded rather cryptically to it over the last couple of calls, he had wanted to wait until the time was right to tell us about it.

He had partnered with a company called Boombotix, which made small speakers that you could plug into your devices. RZA had been pondering the idea of restoring physicality to music in a more practical sense than a multimillion-dollar album and had negotiated a deal where *A Better Tomorrow* was actually embedded into the speaker itself. This opened up twin avenues for innovation—one was to restore the idea of owning a physical incarnation of music in the form of a speaker. The other was an antipiracy measure.

Priced at around the eighty dollar mark, you would be able to buy a limited edition of *A Better Tomorrow* pressed into the hardware with Wu-Tang artwork on the face. The speaker would play other music, but you couldn't play the embedded music on any other system. Both as a gift for those who supported the physicality of the medium and as an antipiracy experiment, two extra tracks appeared on the Boombotix release of *A Better Tomorrow*, tracks that you couldn't get either on CD or through digital stores. And to this day, as I write this . . . those tracks still haven't leaked. Fair fucking play to the Abbot—the symbol was spawning real-world applications. I ordered a bottle of Limoncello.

The waiters didn't seem to be in any great hurry to get rid of us—we'd been there for three hours already, but we were cheery enough and they seemed happy to let us settle in for the next item on the agenda, what would become known as Plan B.

If the name of the plan didn't exactly set the imagination ablaze, absolutely everything else about it did. Cilvaringz had the floor. And it went a little something like this . . .

We would set a cutoff date for Paddle8 to try selling the album and keep the contractual limits of our deal with them very tight. If we went on a fresh offensive in January or February, after *A Better Tomorrow* had taken center stage, we would give them six months tops, because if it hadn't sold by then, with all the press and all the publicity, it probably wasn't going to.

Honesty wasn't an option, which says as much about reception as conception, but having got this far, there could be no admission of failure. So we would fake a sale if it didn't legitimately sell. It would be complex, as with Paddle8 in the mix, we would have to "sell" it as if by magic shortly after our contract with them expired, with no third party to confirm the reality of the sale, which would doubtless raise all kinds of suspicions in Paddle8's boardroom. Or we actually had to buy the fucking thing from ourselves and swallow the commission paid to Paddle8. I had my doubts about how keen Mr. S would be to buy back his own investment at "retail" prices. But we could figure all this out. The bottom line was, we would create a "buyer" character in this story.

But say the investor did buy it back, pretending all the while to Paddle8 that he was for real and paying all too real a commission. How did that help anything beyond declaring the concept a success? How did that help Mr. S? You couldn't commercialize the album, so what—was he going to take it on tour? Were we going to make the money back through exhibitions? That would be a whole new layer of logistical clusterfuck.

Cilvaringz was way ahead of me. We couldn't be seen to put the album on any kind of release after all the rhetoric about the single-copy concept. We'd be crucified, and telling us to go fuck ourselves would be an understandably cathartic moment for all those fans who felt betrayed. We couldn't sell it. But the buyer could. Especially with a few theatrical embellishments.

If we were to reinforce the fact that the album could not be used for commercial purposes in the press when the time was right, we could kill two birds with one stone. First, we would galvanize the mystique around the album by hammering home that the music was designed not to see the light of day through any traditional routes and remove the profit incentive from the sale. It would make the sale far harder to pitch, but it would set the concept in reinforced steel.

Second, if someone did buy it through Paddle8, it could be for no other motive than to enjoy it as a work of art and share it with the world through exhibition if the buyer so chose. He could sell tickets to a listening exhibition, and he retained the right to give it away online for free, as it would have been churlish to strangle that last hope. But what were the chances of anyone actually doing that after spending millions to be the only listener? Either way, it tightened the integrity of what I guess we were now calling Plan A.

First we'd eliminate any chance of a commercial entity buying it, and if that wasn't enough, we'd slap on an eighty-eight-year noncommercialization embargo so the public wouldn't have a chance to hear it in their lifetime. We needed to do something along these lines anyway to dissuade our commercial suitors and clarify what a "sole copy" actually meant, but this could now serve a twin purpose. By playing up ourselves as pantomime villain, and confronting the public with the reality of losing music as a result of the new economics, we were laying the groundwork for a hero to appear, a man of the people. It was a psychological chess game worthy of that old Florentine son, Niccolò

Machiavelli. And the key to it was embedding a loophole in a seemingly final clause. Which Cilvaringz already had locked down.

Eighty-eight years felt like a nice round number to place on the noncommercialization clause. The clause was tenuous, as eighty-eight years was actually longer than copyright time frames in law, but it had the symbolic advantage of allowing everyone to picture a general release in the twenty-second century—the unveiling of a time capsule that would unleash a frozen moment from the golden age of hip-hop onto a whole new society. Having spent decades under lock and key, the album might see the dawn of a new century, and neither buyer nor seller would be alive to see it, just our respective descendants. You can't say that doesn't have a certain ring to it.

Having built this impregnable wall against release, we would then invite our newly crowned and entirely illusory Plan B "hero" to breach the living shit out of it. He would hold a press conference to say he'd heard the album, realized it couldn't be locked in a vault, and spent the next month putting our noncommercialization clause under sustained assault. He would discover the chink in the armor, announce he had found the loophole in our contractual prohibition, and take it to the people in triumph. The public savior of the album offering a once in a lifetime opportunity.

So what was the loophole going to be? Well, the buyer couldn't commercialize the music, but he did have certain merchandising rights. But instead of T-shirts and mugs, he would press up thirty-six thousand gorgeously packaged CDs and put them on sale for a hundred dollars each. Only thing was, all the CDs would be blank, containing none of the interdicted musical content, and thus no more than a beautifully designed medium, being sold as merchandise.

The music would remain in escrow with a trusted third party who would sell the albums—no one was going to start throwing money at some unknown businessman on the promise of music down the line (faking a buyer and preserving secrecy offered a very small pool of candidates). So we needed some way to bank the money that people would feel comfortable with.

If the thirty-six thousand CDs didn't sell, then the buyer would keep the album private and the public would lose its only chance to hear it. But if all thirty-six thousand copies did sell within a limited time frame of six weeks, then the music would be released for free to the people who bought the CD, but only after the benchmark was reached. That was built-in piracy protection. Once you'd made your money back, who cared if it was pirated, and by making the thirty-six thousand copies limited-edition numbered prints, you could guarantee that the owners would be reluctant to stick the music online themselves, as evidenced by the Bundle Experiments discussed earlier.

Having pitted buyer against seller, the second act would need to ramp up the drama. We would have to denounce him in the press and pretend to instigate a lawsuit preventing him from executing his nefarious plan until the question of whether selling packaging on a promise of music to come qualified as commercialization could be settled in court. If we could spit fire and hurl threats while he raised his trusty sword to defend the public against the nasty ol' Clan, we would have some proper Hollywood shit on our hands.

And then, when the thirty-six-thousandth copy sold, all the packaging would be mailed out with an individual code in each.

A website would appear online where, upon the successful entry of the code, the music could be downloaded and burned to the CD in the package, making it an official album with case, printed CD, and music.

After a respectable interval in the doghouse, we would then reveal that it had all been part of a master plan. Five media outlets would receive a leather portfolio containing a date, a time, and a Web address. And at those coordinates, a video would appear.

It would be a homage to *The Usual Suspects*. A quote from Al Jazeera about the album would fade into a black screen as rising strings set the scene. *"In subverting industry standards—an artist making an album that might never be heard and being paid the lion's share of profits—Wu-Tang Clan also appears to be making a deal with the devil. It is, however, the devil they know."*

A journalist sits in his chair, perusing the press clippings and asking Cilvaringz how he feels about having been outwitted by the buyer after he and RZA had gone to such lengths to keep the album from being released. Cilvaringz takes umbrage at his tone and storms out. Closing the book on the saga, the journalist takes one last look through the story's archive when he suddenly notices a new picture among the press clippings. It could only have been placed there by Cilvaringz. On examining it, he sees what is unmistakably a photo of Cilvaringz and the fake buyer with their arms around each other . . . dated 2006. Suddenly realizing that the entire story had been an illusion spun over years, he gasps, drops his coffee, leaps up, and gives chase as the soundtrack explodes in climax.

As the hapless journalist bursts through the lobby, Cilvaringz steps out into the street toward a waiting black Jaguar. Clad head to toe in a chauffeur uniform and driving away . . . is the buyer. And in the back? RZA with the box.

Questioning everything, the journalist rushes back to his office, opens his computer, and sees the words PRESS PLAY. The scene cuts to Kevin Spacey leaning over a desk, radiating all the spine-crawling menace of Frank Underwood and Keyser Söze together as the music drops to silence. Eyes piercing the lens, he says, "The greatest trick ever pulled in the history of music . . . was convincing the world this album would disappear . . . and like that . . . it is done."

As a drumroll thunders and a smirk spreads across his face, he raps his signet ring on the table twice and the film fades to black . . . then, the Wu logo. And underneath, the words THE SEAL . . . THE ART OF THEATER.

Cilvaringz stopped talking. Silence. I couldn't decide if it was suicidal lunacy or pure genius, but whatever the fuck it was and however well or shockingly advised we'd be to consider it, it would certainly be an extraordinary piece of theater. There were nagging flaws, like reattaching value to packaging and giving music away for free, which contradicted the original concept, and I wasn't comfortable with suggesting we'd planned to fake the sale all along, but this was some grand sweeping shit and it ticked so many symbolic boxes. If anyone ever trusted us again long enough to acknowledge them.

It brought the drama back to the increasingly stale dynamics of album releases, reattaching an experiential value to music. It created a distribution model that limited piracy by releasing content only after a desired benchmark was reached. It brought physicality back to music on a macro scale. The physical copies would hold and possibly even appreciate in value as rarities and part of a notorious public story. That meant everyone shared the upsides, including the artist, who would have the power to set his own price. And we would have escaped the single-copy concept unscathed—or at least as unscathed as could be, depending on how much the public loved or hated us for playing them like a harlequin hustler. Cilvaringz hoped the grandeur of executing a complex, multilayered play over a period of years would outweigh any concerns about the methods employed.

We needed another bottle of Limoncello. And the plotting motherfucker didn't even drink.

BAROQUE 'N' ROLL

The next few months were a gentle flurry of admin as we and Paddle8 herded ducks into a row. It was a time of process, designing a framework for presentation and sale while sifting through a detailed reality.

The idea of a standalone auction featuring only the album was alluring. It would concentrate energy into a defined climax and act as a connector, synthesizing the art and music worlds. Part conference, part spectacle, part mixer for the creative industries, it had the potential to not only be the party of the year, but a genuine opportunity for engagement. Set in an abandoned factory or some similarly gritty ode to industrial aesthetics, we could potentially run the whole event as an installation. Creation and renewal in manufacturing's grave.

Well, I was brought down in no uncertain terms by Gabriel. He had become a real confidant of late, and our perception of him and Paddle8 had gone from being business and conceptual partners to something deeper—a true feeling of togetherness. We began factoring the way any of our moves might blow back on Paddle8 into our decisions, and there was a burgeoning swell of team spirit. There was less polite pussyfooting and a lot more real talk, and unfortunately, my vision of a phoenix rising from the industrial ashes sipping Dom Perignon and charting new directions for art and music fell victim to the new up-frontness.

The reality was that you couldn't just auction off the album. That would require people to bid for it and then go home with a binding sale. Problem was that it was far from clear to people what they were bidding on, and it was even less clear to their lawyers. What did they actually own, what rights would they have, and what recourse would they have if we fucked them on the deal? The unique nature of the album meant that a new legal framework would have to be established with an interested party before he parted with his cash.

It was all very well for us to sit down and try to draw up an overarching legal contract that could be inspected alongside the sales catalog before anyone bid for anything. But you couldn't really construct such a framework without an opposing side raising their concerns and laying down what protections and rights they wanted. It would be a balancing act between what we could surrender and what they could live with, and that would vary between individuals. We couldn't present a contract as a fait accompli, but would have to hammer it out with the buyer and his legal team on a case by case basis. Which also added the fascinating dimension of the buyer playing a role in the new realities, an active participant in deciding the final context of the album and the genesis of the business model.

So a private sale it would have to be. I was a bit gutted, though. It would be difficult to create the same kind of nuclear drama with a slow process out of the public eye, but history doesn't always bend to your will. I wasn't even unduly worried about trumpeting an auction and ending up with no bids, as we'd had enough nibbles already to reassure, and when you inject stage-craft and alcohol into proceedings, reticence can only slip. But private sale it was—and that made some kind of coming-out event even more critical. It was one thing announcing an auction date in the press and steering the crescendo toward that, entirely another getting people to go and have behind-the-scenes conversations with Paddle8. We'd have to do an exhibition of some sort in New York in the New Year. We could even resurrect my factory plan, but whatever happened, we had to do something and stamp Paddle8's name all over it so people knew who to talk to.

Paddle8 began putting together a password-protected micro-site that would act as a digital catalog for the sale. Our instinct was to prefer a physical catalog, all glossy and shit, but Gabriel again raised an excellent point. Sale catalogs went to established collectors of a certain genre. Who the fuck were we going to send this to? This was an "if you build it they will come" scenario, and once we'd built it, we needed international access for anyone and everyone who might be into this. This might sell to someone who'd never bought a piece of art in their lives and consequently wasn't on any mailing lists. It was a slight contradiction using the digital to sell the physical, but then we weren't on some grumpy crusade to turn back the clocks. We wanted timeless values in an evolving world and a fluid balance between the tangible and the virtual. Utilizing digital techniques was a key part of that.

On September 9, 2014, another revolutionary music story broke. U2 released their thirteenth album, *Songs of Innocence,* to five hundred million people for free through a tie-in with Apple. Within seconds, all hell broke loose.

Now, I'd argue that jumping into bed with a corporation is never the way to go, even one with such extraordinarily strong brand identity as Apple. I mean, I am a Mac addict, I love their design and clean lines, I even thought the backlit logo on the laptops was a stroke of genius. But Apple is equally notorious for using sweatshops and for being really up their own asses about compatibility. The whole iPod not connecting to a PC thing when it first came out, iTunes leasing rather than selling music, trying to reinvent the headphone jack, changing the fucking shape of SIM cards. They had some major control issues—that much was evident, so for someone, especially the self-proclaimed Saint Bono, to bring all that baggage into their album release was already symbolically questionable.

And then, of course, there was the small matter of the NSA distribution model. On what planet did anyone in either the U2 or the Apple camp think that it was going to be a win to force an album onto people's devices? People curate their playlists; they use them as a kind of digital stand-in for a record collection and generally see them as an expression of individual identity. Dropping an album someone didn't volunteer for into that heady cocktail of technology and personality was invasive at best and Orwellian at worst.

If we had limited choice through price, they had suffocated it entirely. And worse still, in clumsy, totalitarian style the fucking thing was impossible to delete. We were living in a post-Snowden world where control through digital technology was a major issue, and by highlighting public impotence in the face of a corporate deal, they were actively denying people individual identity. *Songs of Innocence?* There was nothing innocent about any of this.

And then, as if to emphasize his long-standing divorce from reality, Bono made a point of saying that the only thing that mattered was for the music to be heard. Sure, if you're U2 and one of the most lucrative touring bands on the planet. But try telling that to the guy with a guitar, some scrawled lyrics, and a dream. Where's the economic framework for him to survive? Being heard may nourish the soul, but it doesn't nourish much else, and it felt deeply irresponsible for a role model like Bono to tell people that it was okay for music to be free—both from a struggling artist's perspective and because of the kind of blessing it gave to entitlement culture. It just isn't healthy for society to feel entitled to music, even less so when the medium is a company famed for overpricing its products. It's okay to spend thousands of dollars on a Mac, but not okay to spare a couple of bucks for an independent artist.

Forget capitalism; anarchism is a beautiful thing. Not the anarchism you see in the media, where people fling Molotov cocktails at the police behind hysterical news graphics, but philosophical anarchism, which is about self-governing communities. The only way an anarchic community, or indeed any other community, truly works is if everyone contributes and supports one another—be it through barter, collaboration, or some medium of exchange. You loved a song someone sang so you cook them dinner. You don't just enjoy their song, then disregard them entirely as they cook you dinner. That isn't community, that's ugly. It should be a point of pride and actively enhance the experience of music to help pay for it and not just be told that a corporation would tuck you in and bring you presents paid for behind the scenes through God knows what means. That was a surrender of control, of identity, of morality, and of dignity. What the fuck were they up to?

You have to ask yourself how much Apple paid U2 for a five-week exclusive, over and above the $100 million they spent on "marketing." They marketed their way straight to howling abuse—getting absolutely slaughtered in the press and on social media, something that made us fully appreciate how open the world had been to our concept. This was a bloodbath. Apple rolling out an app to delete the album three weeks later was the final epitaph to the experiment. I guess it just goes to show what happens when you put two messiah complexes in a room.

AND THEN THERE WERE TWO

A Better Tomorrow was finally finished and slated for release on December 2, 2014. It had been a torrid ride and there had been myriad moments of hand-wringing despair, wondering if it would ever happen. But despite the personal, creative, and financial disagreements that had played out in the spotlight, peace had finally been made among the elders. There was a huge sigh of relief all round, both at the Wu Music Group (RZA's company, which was handling the release) and in our virtual HQ, the conference call chamber.

Despite the fact that scheduling had been at the mercy of the fates, counterbalancing the single-copy concept with a public album was vital. This had all been nailed down before my involvement, but the flip side of the confusion created by two different albums following two different paths was an ongoing musical dialogue with the fans. It would have been far harder to justify making an album private without having a public one in the mix, and as a group remaining true to their people, launching the single-copy album alone would have been a kick in the teeth too far. This was a perfect equilibrium.

Not that you'd have known it on some of the fan forums. Before *A Better Tomorrow* had even been released, we started to see a flood of vitriol pouring in from those who had already drawn imaginary comparisons between two albums they'd never heard. It was a fascinating insight into the psychology of access and provided some compelling data for one aspect of our experiment.

One question was fundamental. If you are making an album that you know may to all intents and purposes remain private, how hard are you really going to try? Are you going to put as much care and effort into convincing one person as you would into an album that stands or falls on how many people vote with their wallets? Not to mention that up until this point, the musical content of *Once Upon a Time in Shaolin* had swerved any kind of critical examination or review. So if no critic and only one fan would ever hear it, maybe it was a gimmick with some recycled B-sides.

So if you are a fan and feeling a little cheated, would you console yourself with this logic, nurture a closer affinity to the public album, and create a soothing scenario in your head where the single-copy aberration is a pile of shit? And the buyer probably wouldn't know jack about hip-hop anyway? I think I might have taken this road myself; it's a pretty classic psychological reflex: if you aren't invited to the party, convince yourself that it will be terrible and that everyone who is going must be a dick.

And yet a huge number of people had arrived at the exact opposite conclusion. By their logic, *Once Upon a Time in Shaolin* shimmered with a mystical glow—it was the holy grail of albums, a sacred trust, and some of the Clan's best work, while *A Better Tomorrow* had been cobbled together in a whirlwind of conflict and was being used to palm off the fans with an unsatisfactory pat on the head.

It didn't help that we had flagged *Once Upon a Time* as the classic Wu sound of the nineties, a period every fan could agree on while musical progression may not carry the majority. People are always chasing the sound that first hooked them. Ask almost any band how changing direction worked for them and I guarantee they'll tell a similar story.

It fed straight back into the questions of access, exclusivity, and mystery. The less we played any music, the more some people projected their idealized sound onto it. By cloaking the album in so much mystique, we had opened the door for imaginations to run free, and knowing that they wouldn't be subject to anything as conventional as actually listening to it, wave after wave of fans took the baton and ran with it toward their vision of the perfect album.

Everyone wanted the one they couldn't have. Never mind that *A Better Tomorrow* had taken years and was infused with the latest musical symphonies, it was going to be available to everyone, so who cares. It's that other one I want. The one you say I can't have.

Jesus—talk about proving a point. We saw this reaction in by no means everyone and our sample group were the kind of diehard fans that hit the forums rather than the more casual collectors, so the results had been skewed to a certain degree, but fucking hell: there were a lot of people who thought that way. It really did come down to "Well, I can have this one anytime I like, so who gives a fuck. I can't have that one, so let me put it on a pedestal."

Access breeds indolence. Interdiction breeds desire. We've

always fantasized about the forbidden fruit; it doesn't come much more archetypal than the Book of Genesis. The one thing we cannot touch is what we lust after insatiably. And then, once we've laid hands upon it and dragged it down to earth from the imagined dazzle of the heavens, it loses its halo, and we scan the horizon for our next conquest, like some twisted prince in search of a virgin.

We had instructed Paddle8 to keep their foot off the gas while *A Better Tomorrow* geared up for release, but they understandably wanted to test the water with a couple of clients they could rely on to maintain discretion. Conversations were held on a surface level, revolving largely around price, a vague sense of the rights and restrictions, and sheer curiosity to find out more. How involved had RZA been, what was Cilvaringz's pedigree to be driving this project, what did it sound like, and so on.

We hadn't announced that Paddle8 was our partner yet, so the exploratory phase played out within a very tight circle of people they dealt with regularly. But one issue was already sharpening to a sticking point. Absolutely no one was prepared to put an offer on the table for private use without having listened to at least some of the album. Mystique only goes so far, and these guys didn't get rich by making rash purchases of unknown entities, sight unseen.

Here was another irony. Interest was still being expressed in buying the album as a commercial vehicle, and those parties didn't seem to care too much about what the music actually sounded like. They sounded pretty confident that it would recoup their investment on the hype alone, and even though that $5 million offer had specified a film licensing deal without the buyer's having heard any of the music, you got the impression that putting a banner across the top corner of a movie poster saying "includes previously unheard tracks from *Once Upon a Time in Shaolin*" would act as an effective marketing tool whether it gelled with the film scenes or not.

But conversations with people who were already aware of the commercial embargo were taking a much more studied direction. If you couldn't realistically make your money back, then suddenly the essence of what you were buying mattered a whole lot more. It was no longer just a commodity but something you were paying millions to live with. What if it sucked?

Gabriel was clear as day. The only way this was going to work was if we found a way to securely play excerpts of the album to serious buyers. We were equally adamant that they would have to be studiously vetted in advance to make sure we didn't get some blogger masquerading as a billionaire ripping the audio through a concealed transmitter. It would have to happen on a case-by-case basis, and we wouldn't leave a copy of the excerpts anywhere. We would have to upload it to a website, make it available for a limited time, and have security in the room where the listening session was taking place.

Only two people had ever heard the album in its entirety, RZA and Cilvaringz. Not even the mixing or mastering engineers. The Clan had all heard the segments they were individually involved in. And me? Well, with a mixture of purity, integrity, and breathtaking hypocrisy, I simply didn't want to hear it. Which saved RZA and Cilvaringz from having to lie about only two people ever having listened to it when a third had actually gotten ears on the whole thing.

I have lost count of the number of people who asked if I had heard it and when I told them I didn't want to, either thought I was nuts or, more likely, that I wasn't allowed to and was covering my impotence with the old "well, I didn't want to anyway" chestnut. The thing is, I was never a big hip-hop guy, so the nuances would be lost and I'd never be able to judge how good or bad it was. But the real reason I never once asked to listen to it? I didn't want it to become real.

Now that might sound like hypocrisy of the highest order when set against the musings on the psychology of access above. But psychology isn't something that other people do—it's universal. I was deep into an idea and a set of abstractions all paradoxically built around the concept of tangibility. It was all about making the music magic again, and yet I was terrified to listen in case it lost its magic. My greatest fear was that seeing it morph from ideas and energy into actual sound waves would damage my own perception of it to the point that I might never recover my passion. And if that went out the window, then sincerity wouldn't be far behind.

None of us wanted to lie, either. There were enough questions about the nuts and bolts of this project without introducing an element of conscious deceit. This thing lived or died on its integrity, and once ruptured, forever lost.

Yet Gabriel was pushing us further. He insisted that the critics had to hear this. He was immovable on this question, and by this point, all the secrecy we'd immersed ourselves in had bottomed out into a bunker mentality. It had taken so much to protect this record that the thought of opening it up to critics who might have an agenda, who didn't like the idea, who didn't like the Clan—whatever—filled us with abject horror. Wouldn't that erode the mystery?

Well, again, mystique has its limits. This album was about as real as the digital paper the media stories were printed on. At some point we had to establish its musical credentials, and we couldn't do it through the public alone. We needed the voices of the critical press if this was ever going to be fully credible as a piece of music and not simply a beguiling phantom.

So the exhibition we already had penciled in for the New Year would have to include the critics. We would have to play at least some of the music there, and we would need a sampler for serious buyers to check out. But no one was going to listen to the whole thing until the eventual buyer became the third person in the world to hear it. The debate over how long a sampler should be then began to rage. Five minutes or forty-five minutes? What was the Goldilocks dose?

And speaking of exhibitions, what was going on in Cambridge, Massachusetts? Where were we with our much-vaunted Harvard debate?

TEMPTATION

Doubts were creeping in on both sides. While debating the full spectrum of issues in the cradle of American intellectual life retained an undisputed appeal, the nagging question of context and elitism loomed ever larger. The deal breaker for Harvard was that some of the music should be played. And wouldn't you know it; that was our deal breaker, too. Having arrived at the point where we knew we would only hold a single listening, we had to wonder if Harvard was really the most appropriate forum for that fleeting peek behind the veil.

Rightly or wrongly, it would inevitably raise questions about why only students at the country's most elite university had the opportunity to hear some of the record. The event would have been open only to students, faculty, and a handful of reporters, which on a less noble level wouldn't do much for the album's profile in the one and only listening session. It didn't even feel like we could do two, one there and one in New York, because again, if you're going to do a second, why not L.A., why not Paris, why not London . . . why Harvard? It just didn't feel like the right move.

We had done a degree of groundwork in establishing the

logistics for a listening session at Harvard, with PMC, the company that built the speakers the album was mastered on, offering to fly a pair out so the listening could be curated through the same balance of lovingly crafted physics the album was brought to life on.

But the whole event was starting to feel like a red herring, albeit a tempting one. It just felt too blazers and privilege. Which may be totally unfair, but it wasn't about convincing us, it was about how the symbolism would be interpreted. And it turned out that feet were turning cold there too.

The powers that be were definitely pulling a Sotheby's. After the first flush of media glory, in which high-profile professors had leapt aboard and a huge auditorium in the business school was being booked, the sponsoring professor was no longer answering e-mails and we were being sold a new venue in the hip-hop archive. I was pretty taken aback to discover Harvard even had a hip-hop archive, and I was torn between admiration for their engagement with contemporary currents and the incongruity of the words *Harvard* and *hip-hop* in the same sentence. I mean, it was fantastic, but somehow it just felt unconvincing— and dare I say it, it just felt too white to hold our only listening session there. The business school was at least breaking boundaries and tabling the album as a far reaching issue. The hip-hop archive was pigeon holing in a mahogany cubicle.

And anyway, the hip-hop archive was the equivalent of David Redden's music memorabilia auction, while the business school, despite the overriding economic association, was still a headline player. Paul, the postgrad student who had conceived the whole idea, had been fantastic throughout, but we all knew we were reaching the point where we'd have to hug, shake hands, and part ways.

While the conservative bastions of tradition and prestige continued to meet rather than defy expectations, over on the phones, the corporate world was determined not to be left behind in the expectation-meeting sweepstakes.

Creative agencies are a funny old breed. Their job is to have innovative, outside the box ideas on behalf of corporations, bringing a brand together with a dynamic publicity vehicle in a marriage of convenience. Don't have the cash to jump out of a rocket at the edge of space? Meet Red Bull.

It all makes perfect sense, and there is an endless stream of seriously cool shit that would never see the light of day without corporate funding and visionary creative agencies. But I still felt that the slightest sniff of branding would diminish the album and the idea beyond recognition. I'd rather fall flat on our own terms than take thirty pieces of sterile silver.

We had been approached by a creative agency that wanted to pitch us and then Samsung in turn to bring us together on a mutually beneficial project. The agency had an idea, and it was a vast improvement on the last "give away a track for free with our product" kindergarten bullshit. This was far better thought through and tuned to hit all our sweet spots while offering Samsung the chance to propose something a little bit more credible than a straight giveaway. Guerrilla marketing for the discerning conglomerate.

They would fund an epic video. We would have total creative control; we could make it as lavishly cinematic as we wanted, as conceptual as we wished, and as revolutionary as our imaginations would permit. It didn't need to stop at one track, it could be a fifteen-minute video set to a medley of music from the album, a distilled essence of feeling channeled through the alchemy of cinema.

The video would then tour the world as an installation. There would be no digital trace—no YouTube, no website embeds, just a succession of galleries, exhibition spaces, and museums. It would redefine perceptions of the music video, create a new inclusivity by allowing people from across the world to experience *Once Upon a Time in Shaolin* in a meaningful way, while still preserving the entire record for the buyer to be the third person in the world to hear. It solved the problem of listening to the album in an exhibition space with nothing but a clinical white wall for company. It stayed true to our concept in every single possible way. Except one.

I'm probably setting myself up here for hate mail, general vilification, and plenty of "who the fuck is this prick anyway and how fucking dare he sabotage people's chances to see and hear this." Sorry, guys.

Much to the annoyance of everyone else, I immediately advised against it. I didn't have anything resembling a deciding vote—that was RZA and Cilvaringz's prerogative—but having come this far in harmony, our executive board liked to agree on things rather than spiral into discord. I just could not deal with the idea of Samsung's name anywhere near the film, the event, or anything whatsoever. PMC flying speakers out for a listening was a form of sponsorship, no doubt, but they were a small, family-owned company, and all they wanted was for us to tell the truth about how much we valued their sound and how they had legitimately been a part of the journey. That wasn't the same as "Samsung Presents."

Which is no disrespect to Samsung—I'd have felt the same about any brand in this particular project, as I've pontificated on before. But this was excruciating because it was such a fucking great idea. Full respect to the creative agency behind it—it was an incredibly classy pitch and demonstrated in surround sound just how much they'd understood the music-as-art concept.

I'd rather have raised the money through crowdfunding or silent investors like Mr. S, but he wasn't overly keen, either, for a very different set of reasons. His first question to me when I put it to him was "How does this affect our timeline?"

He had a point. This could take years, and where did that leave the album? It would be a huge operation, booking galleries months, sometimes years in advance, bringing in airport-style security at each, and then a plunge into the whirlpool of unforeseen issues that anything like this inevitably raised. And he laid down the decisive line.

Now, I don't know if he was playing us while protecting his investment or he was genuinely so engrossed in this project that he really did believe in its integrity above its bottom line, but his final comment echoed through the chambers.

"Surely this is back to giving music away for free. You make the music-as-art statement beautifully. You create personal and emotional value, but the economics don't stack up, and thus, the statement about the economic value of music is dead in the water. You would spend several hundred thousand dollars making a video, you would struggle to make that plus the costs of the venue hire, security, transport, etc. back without making tickets absurdly expensive and you still have an album that hasn't sold because everyone is going to these gallery screenings. It's yet another sacrifice in the name of art."

This was why I liked working with this guy. He knew perfectly well that I didn't give too much of a fuck about his investment and that the way to our hearts was through concept rather than balance sheets. This could be some magnificently manipulative bullshit to get us back on track. But hustle or not, he was right. People would assume that the ticket prices were realizing a handsome return, but unless we wanted to actually distribute it to hundreds of galleries simultaneously and "open on a thousand screens" this was going to be a long, costly affair that made one point at the expense of the other.

And you couldn't do multiple screenings at different times—it was just lame and way too much like movie distribution to feel fresh. There were only two options that worked. One was to do them all at the same time on the same day across continents and make it a global event. The clock strikes midnight in New York, 5 a.m. in London, and 1 p.m. in Tokyo. And the world shared an experience as one. *Once Upon a Time in Shaolin,* the world united.

Fucking brilliant. And yet prohibitive because of both the investment required and the length of time it would take to set up in carefully chosen locations. Every single gallery would need to be free at the same time, people needed to be convinced to open at weird hours—it would be a major operation.

The only other option was to move from city to city in procession as excitement circumnavigated the globe. It would be a nomadic wandering, the album's shamanic voyage around the world. It would feel like an actual tour, and always radiate the excitement of the circus coming to town. But again, it would take months if not years to organize. It wasn't about booking obvious event spaces—it was about booking highly individual venues that would amplify the experience through their own symbolism. If we were going to do it, we had to do it right. But, heartbreakingly, everyone had other commitments, and we couldn't just take two years off to organize a loss-making exhibition. And God only knew how long the film would take to cast, shoot, edit. It was an impossible dream.

Samsung might pay for all this if they came fully aboard and the creative agency in the midst of the discussion could excite them as much as they'd excited us. But then we would have gone from a band of brothers working toward a shared goal to being in bed with a behemoth sporting its own agenda. The potential loss of control was all encompassing. Losing control of a project, even fractionally, after so many years—it was too big a risk. And at the final reckoning, it still, in the immortal words of Mr. S, would allow the artistic yin of our concept to break the circle and ditch the economic yang.

We said no. And it fucking hurt. And then, in the spirit of synchronicity . . . a director called.

It was Nabil Elderkin, one of the most cinematic music video directors in the game. It felt like an urgent nudge from fate to get back on the video track, but it turned out that Nabil had his own video in mind.

He was in Morocco shooting a video for the Skrillex single "Fuck That" and wanted to know if the album casing could be included in some way. I was in London, RZA was off shooting a movie, but Cilvaringz was in Marrakech and keen to get involved with Nabil's plan. The Skrillex project starred *La Haine*'s Saïd Taghmaoui and was clearly set to outshine your average music video. I was uncomfortable with the title—I didn't really want anything of ours to be associated with something called "Fuck That"—but RZA felt that the blurring of lines between dance music and hip-hop and the guest appearance of the box in the video would be an intriguing, yet suitably cryptic twist.

The video was a superb piece of work. God only knows what relationship it had to the track; I'm positive Nabil just made the film he wanted to make. It was a story of a rather intense street fighter who punches his way to some kind of redemption. Not everyone is entirely happy with him, though—maybe he was supposed to throw the fight or maybe he'd fucked someone's daughter, but he is kidnapped and taken into the desert, where a shadowy cabal of warriors appear holding a shining silver ark. They are holding the album.

We'd agreed to blur out the *W* so the box remained an Easter egg in the video, and its use throughout was fitting, tasteful, and creatively interesting. Only thing was, these tribal warriors, these Sahara samurai, suddenly looked worryingly like fucking ISIS. No one had made the connection during the shoot, as they were supposed to be these mystical ancients straight out of the book of storytelling archetypes, but now, watching back the final cut . . . ouffff.

Before we knew it, our CD cover was being labeled as a silver copy of the Koran with demonic powers and those charming turbaned chaps were being depicted as foamingly homicidal Islamic militants. They really did look like fucking ISIS, though. Shit. Cue the PR crisis.

I could picture the meltdown. Skrillex would take a whole heap of shit, but then Cilvaringz would suddenly be back in the spotlight. Who the fuck was this Cilvaringz guy anyway? What's this whole connection with Morocco been about? Maybe Cilvaringz was a secret ISIS supporter and all-around nasty-ass motherfucker. What if he was trying to convert the Wu? And why was he using this album as propaganda to glorify ISIS?

Ironically enough, we were saved by the press. The media's taste for hysteria is matched only by its addiction to gossip, and a readily available tidbit trumped the effort of fomenting a moral panic. Someone on the Wu-Tang forum must have heard something about a Skrillex connection, because they stormed onto a thread and declared that Skrillex had bought the album. And Cilvaringz, jokingly, said "Yup."

The next thing we knew, the website Highsnobiety had announced Skrillex as the buyer of the album, and it wasn't long before *Complex* rolled out the "scoop," too, albeit with a few more layers of skepticism built in. No doubt they fretted about a competitor beating them to the headline, but the story went live before any requests for comment had been answered. Virality was pretty much hardwired into the image of Skrillex as buyer, and to our immense relief, the only Skrillex–Cilvaringz headline taking light was a good old American capitalism story rather than outrage at the video.

I'd love to credit us with the kind of Machiavellian cunning that had me as the original forum poster under a false name and Cilvaringz saying "Yup" in a carefully calibrated plan to throw the press onto a different scent, but alas, I can't. And the accidental reality was more fun anyway. Instead of a crisis, we had fresh evidence of how big a story this album was—we had gone months since the last round of press, but at the tiniest hint of unverified gossip, the carousel was off again. Didn't hurt being associated with a high-profile musician as buyer, but seriously, guys, even I know it wouldn't be Skrillex's style to buy this—it just didn't fit any aspect of his personality.

Still—no one was going to look this particular gift horse in the mouth. Thank Allah . . . I mean *Highsnobiety*. ;-)

2015 dawned bright and full of promise. RZA was gearing up to direct his new film *Coco,* Cilvaringz was awaiting the birth of his second child, and I was still chuckling about having turned up to my daughter Zara's birthday party pretending to be her long-lost Russian uncle Vladimir. Life was good, *A Better Tomorrow* was out, *Once Upon a Time in Shaolin* was living the high life at the Royal Mansour, and Paddle8 was setting all systems to go.

We had settled on a password-protected website to act as the album's sale catalog. RZA and Alexander were drawing up personal introductions, interviews were being conducted to give some deeper insight to the concept, rare photos of the Clan from Jonathan Mannion's archive were being collated, and Chris Norris, RZA's coauthor on *The Tao of Wu,* was preparing a background article for the site.

With the site in the hands of the design team, attention swung to our one and only exhibition. Gabriel had prepared a list of galleries in New York that we could use as a venue for a listening session, and as we sat down to consider their virtues, a sense of unease began to pervade the sunshine.

Sweeping Statement No. 23,645: Commercial galleries are way too frigid to create genuine atmosphere around a listening session.

Galleries are rather clinical places. I suppose the logic of white walls and unprepossessing modernity is to limit the extent to which context can influence the perception of an artwork. Sure, you have all kinds of different aesthetics, from steampunk to brick, but there is no question that the overwhelming majority are set to a default shade of sensory deprivation. This might be the proven medium to exhibit canvas or sculpture, but it really wouldn't work musically. It just felt—well, emotionless, as the frequencies bounced off the temporary plaster walls and wilted.

We expressed our limited enthusiasm to Gabriel. There was no doubt that the galleries he and the Paddle8 team had sourced were prestigious among the art community, and if it was good enough for Jeff Koons or Damien Hirst, then whether our untrained eyes saw the benefits or not, we would be exhibiting with major players. Yes . . . but no. What about a noncommercial gallery or, better still, a museum of contemporary art?

The problem was that the major public institutions that were sustained by grants and endowments had very clear remits. They were about the experience and appreciation of art, creating a social axis of beauty and ideas that was open to all and acted as a bulwark against the rising tide of monetization. In doing so, they had to maintain a strong separation of church and state, or in this case, commercial and public. The top institutions might be more than happy to exhibit our album, but not if it was identifiably part of a sale campaign. Major museums could not be seen to be co-opted into a PR role for a commercial venture.

On behalf of society, thank God. On behalf of us . . . damn their interminable red tape. But hang on. We were going to sell the thing, but what if a Picasso that was going to be auctioned off in six months and risked disappearing into a vault forever was available for a final exhibition. Would that be okay? Where did you draw the line between public and private interest?

And that was the key. To what extent would hosting the only listening session of this artwork be a public service and to what extent would it be an uncomfortable association by lending institutional weight to a commercial venture? It was going to have to be a judgment call, because you could make a compelling argument either way. Gabriel had his doubts about whether an internationally renowned art gallery would be prepared to risk it, especially with such an unusual artwork. They might face a grilling from the board or a roasting from the press, but either way it was going to have to be a brave decision.

The existing list of venues wasn't looking promising. There was one that we call the Gandalf Gallery to this day because they had this installation of weird porcelain lampshade-type things that looked halfway between a wizard's hat and something a Smurf might wear to a wedding. They had been hung at varying heights, with some dropping to about six inches from the floor. We were welcome to hold our listening session there, but only amid the forest of floppy porcelain hats. The art world might find that kind of thing acceptable, but we certainly didn't. Can you imagine trying to play the album and then discuss it with a straight face while bent into a forty-five-degree angle trying to avoid death by Hogwarts?

At this rate, we were better just fucking off the whole idea of a "gallery gallery" and either resurrecting my idea of an abandoned factory or just grabbing a fucking loft and doing the damn thing there without any official art-world hallmarks. Calls were put in to unconventional venues, including one gorgeous record-ing studio that used to be a music hall. All crushed velvet and Roaring Twenties glamour, it certainly had aesthetic appeal, but it felt too overtly "music" and the owner wanted silly money to let us through the door. He didn't need publicity and he seemed to be under the impression that we would throw six-figure sums around for a couple of hours. He was mistaken.

Hope was beginning to fade and solutions were growing in-creasingly outlandish. The thing with New York was that there were almost too many brilliant, unconventional spaces. It was inertia by gluttony as we lurched from underground bunkers to skyscraper rooftops. Gabriel kept drawing us back to the symbolism—yes, we could do any of these places, but we would lose the resonance of putting an album into an art gallery. If we didn't do it in a recognized art arena, then weren't we just doing a rather typical cool album launch?

It was midnight and I was unconscious. The phone rang. RZA was already on a conference call with Gabriel. The unthinkable had happened. MoMA PS1 was on board. Pending extensive pa-rameters.

From its very inception, PS1 had activism running through its veins. Founded as the Institute for Art and Urban Resources Inc., its mission was to breathe creative life into abandoned build-ings, giving bricks and mortar a new electricity while offering up-and-coming artists a chance to flourish, free from the con-straints of tradition and capital. Site-specific works flooded through the pipeline and a newly liberated consciousness found its home in Long Island City.

As one of the oldest and largest contemporary art institutions in the U.S., PS1 surfed the cutting edge of expression, booting open doors and teasing perception through the cracks, as it imbued the art scene in New York and then the world with a dynamic "now" sense of self. Affiliating with its rather grand new stepmother, the Museum of Modern Art, PS1 continued to probe boundaries and deconstruct rules in the name of experimental integrity. Passing the ultimate test by giving MoMA credibility rather than sacrificing its own, PS1 was rusty perfection for every symbol we hoped to harness.

They did, of course, have a rather glaring dilemma. The perception of this album was walking a tightrope between million-dollar bling and a radical reassessment of the nature of art. PS1 was all for supporting the latter, but didn't want to end up tainted by the former. In order to fulfill their institutional responsibilities, they needed some conditions to be met.

First of all, there had to be some members of the public there. This couldn't be a glorified press conference. Second of all, there needed to be a discussion of the project. And third of all, there couldn't be any kind of reference to its sale. This could be the one and only aural exhibition of the album in the world, but it couldn't be a brand tie-in. Classic, really, that we'd spent all this time avoiding brand tie-ins to preserve our own integrity, and now someone was reticent about aligning themselves with us for the exact same reason. You had to crack a wry smile.

This put the Paddle8 team into a quandary. They had worked tirelessly and gone out on all manner of limbs to get behind this project, but they needed some recognition for it and weren't at all keen to be airbrushed out of the picture. It was a totally fair point, and beyond that, how the fuck was anyone going to know who to talk to about buying the album if we exhibited to an international fanfare without an auction house attached?

RZA solved that problem quick as a flash. We had been preparing to announce our partnership with Paddle8 alongside the exhibition, but if that wasn't going to fly, then the matter was simple. Announce the Paddle8 partnership immediately, get that news out, and then go into the PS1 event with the information already out there. One stumbling block cleared.

Then there was the question of Alexander Gilkes speaking at the event. The PS1 curators didn't see the need for it. In their eyes, all that Alexander's participation could really do was emphasize the commercial nature of this project. But again, it wasn't that simple. From our perspective, Paddle8 were far more than salesmen, they were at the forefront of the very idea PS1 wanted to celebrate, of the art world recognizing the gravitas of music alongside painting and sculpture. They weren't just our brokers, they were our partners, and we stood shoulder to shoulder on this. They represented the art world, we represented the music world, and together we would bring a new rocket to the PS1 launch pad.

Fair enough, said PS1, but under no circumstances could he introduce even the faintest whisper of trade into his speech. The very fact that he was up there representing Paddle8 would be enough to give the company its forward-thinking due, and if he confined himself to broad philosophical strokes, then we were a go.

We got down to the brass tacks of space. MoMA PS1 had this geodesic dome they used as an exhibition space for audiovisual installations and unusual events. It was perfect. A contained, unconventional zone, set apart from the main buildings. It was dark and retained a cozy warmth that was a reassuring counterpoint to our bête noire of *murs blancs*. Only one problem. Didn't domes have shocking acoustics?

I for one was scarred by previous attempts to play loud music in a geodesic dome. Basically, the sound waves bounce around like a pinball machine until all you have is a cacophony of feedback. There were no absorbent angles, no bass traps, just an echo chamber of chaos. And however perfect the surroundings and the symbolism were, if it sounded like shit then what was the point?

Enter Jim Toth. A legend in the world of loudspeaker design and sound installation, Jim was an artist in his own right. From building custom sound systems in world-famous clubs to designing sound fields for unusual environments and special events, he balanced an old-school, mad-scientist, "may have toured with the Grateful Dead" vibe with an impeccable reputation for professionalism. He was in charge of audio in the dome, and from our very first e-mail, we knew we were in safe hands. He had the physics nailed; the carpeting and the lining of the dome would deaden the wave bounce to lift the center, a sweet spot where precision was wrought from impact. A hand-built surround sound system featured eight stacks of speakers in an inward-facing circle. Step inside and you were instantly transported. Step outside and it sounded like shit. A primal ring of sonic power.

This was starting to look like we were on track. From the Gandalf Gallery to PS1 in a week. Time to jump on a plane. The album was coming home to New York City.

VOYAGE

I met Cilvaringz at Heathrow. We had decided to fly to the States together to discuss the mission ahead, and he was traveling heavy, so two was always going to be better than one. His hand luggage contained the three silver boxes that made up the album packaging and a laptop with thirteen minutes of music on it, ready to make its debut at MoMA PS1. A make-or-break piece of luggage if ever I saw one.

Things got off to an inauspicious start. We met with a warm embrace outside Terminal 3. I sucked a last cigarette dry and we strolled toward the Virgin Atlantic check-in desk to formalize the journey. And then things skidded into a sharp left turn.

The lady at the check-in desk raised her eyes in silent apology and broke the news that Cilvaringz had been earmarked for extra security checks. We exchanged a pair of raised eyebrows. What was going on here? Was this straight profiling or was there going to be an issue of some kind? We were sent over to a corner where a forbidding American fellow who looked like he played linebacker in college was brandishing a BlackBerry. He introduced himself. He was from the Department of Homeland Security.

U.S. Homeland Security in a London airport? We braced ourselves for some paranoid, heavy-handed Kafka, but our interrogator turned out to be a thoroughly jovial guy. He ran through the leading questions, what countries in the Middle East have you traveled to recently, that sort of thing. Basically, if you said Syria, Iraq, or even Turkey, which was growing notorious as a jump-off for ISIS recruits, you were going to have a problem. Cilvaringz had toured the Middle East in 2007, but nothing since then. Best not to show him the Skrillex video though, eh?

Everything checked out and Mr. Homeland Security typed a load of classified information into his BlackBerry before bidding us bon voyage. We had already developed a fondness for him, though; he was doing his job while minimizing resentment, and by the end we were chuckling like old friends.

I had a crisis on another project, so I spent three hours in the departure lounge on the phone, yelling myself into everyone's bad books while Cilvaringz edged away and pretended not to know me. Sensible. We boarded the plane, I downed some sleeping pills, and we talked strategy while they failed to work. A number of vodkas later, I finally managed to get some shut-eye while Cilvaringz immersed himself in his laptop.

We began our descent into a winter wonderland. It was March, but the Hudson was frozen and vast expanses of snow glimmered in the evening sun. Soaring through the stratosphere, I felt a surge of optimism erupt from my very core. Totally unwarranted, as it turned out. The second we landed, the shit began to hit the fan.

We would be clearing the boxes through customs. We had left the huge leather one behind for the sake of relative convenience, so what we were left with was the outer silver box, the inner silver box, and the silver CD case. And we had the number for Gary, a customs agent who would meet us on the other side of immigration. We dropped him a line, made sure he was there waiting for us, told him we'd be there in ten minutes, and lined up for the brief formality of passport control.

"Would you step this way please, sir?"

No, not me. Tarik. What the fuck? Hadn't this all been resolved at fucking Heathrow? Apparently not, because he was led off by a brisk gentleman in uniform and deposited in a holding room that looked more like the departure lounge at Islamabad airport than the arrivals lounge at JFK. And his precious cargo was unceremoniously dumped in a pile of bags outside.

I was ushered through to baggage claim, where I hoisted a worthless bag of clothes off the conveyor and swore repeatedly to myself. What if he didn't get in? What was the problem with his paperwork? And how the fuck could I get the box back before someone walked off with it? I suddenly realized just how similar people's hand luggage looked—it was like his bag had landed in a family reunion of nondescript black rectangles.

The TSA were remarkably civil, at least to me, and I was mighty relieved that the guy with the kindly face I'd settled on as my best hope allowed me to take Cilvaringz's bag from the pile of misfit carry-ons that littered the pathway into the holding room. Flooring the accelerator, I waddled off toward customs with it and into the sweet embrace of Gary, our customs agent. I briefed him on Tarik's misguided decision to be Arabic and we resolved to get the box cleared while we waited. We were powerless to help Cilvaringz, but the paperwork we could definitely do.

We registered our desire to declare and a silver-haired chap in uniform beckoned us into a back room. I unpacked the boxes with trembling fingers, gently removed the protective packaging, and stepped back proudly to reveal that we had nothing to hide. The officer looked at it skeptically. "This doesn't correspond to the paperwork," he quipped. "The documentation details a cedar and leather box. So what the hell is this?"

Well, a cedar and leather box it was not. And grabbing a shovel to dig myself deeper, I said, "No, no, officer, three silver boxes."

Not a good move. "What do you mean three boxes? You only have papers for one."

"Ah, yes," I said, pirouetting frantically. "That's because they are all part of the one box. See, look, they all fit inside."

"I don't care if they fit inside Rockefeller Center, you're trying to clear three silver boxes when you have papers for one leather box. This is going to have to be a seizure while you figure it out."

We didn't have time to "figure it out." The fucking exhibition was the day after tomorrow. God only knew what bureaucratic nightmares would ensue if we were parted from the box and it vanished into the inanimate equivalent of the holding room Cilvaringz was currently enjoying.

Flailing, I broke the emergency glass and pressed the MoMA button. After all, what good is a big name institution if you can't drop their name in a crisis?

He paused. "Show me," he said, pointing at a computer. "If you're exhibiting this at PS1, then show me the event in their listings."

Fuck. It wasn't listed because we were keeping it top secret until the day of the event so people couldn't dream up ways to record the audio. This was unraveling fast. Damn us and our insatiable need for secrecy. How ironic would it be if the secret album fell victim to its own secrecy?

Acting all casual, I dug out the e-mail chains instead, praying that they would be enough to convince him that we had a legitimate purpose for our misidentified silver haul and the federal government didn't need to trouble themselves with a seizure.

He considered it. "Okay, well, open up that first box and let's see inside. Where's the key?"

Er. Right. The key. I ransacked the suitcase. No trace of a key. Maybe Cilvaringz had a key?

I dialed his number and in the three seconds he lasted before being told in no uncertain terms to switch his phone off and "respect the process," I managed to glean that the key wasn't in his pocket or even on this continent. He'd sent in the box for polishing before leaving Marrakech, and, well, he hadn't seen the key since. There had been a million things to do and he had been handed a wrapped box. Surely the polisher hadn't forgotten the fucking key.

I swore violently under my breath, ground out a sunny smile, and turned to face the officer.

"You're going to laugh," I said. He didn't look convinced.

He took it better than I feared. By this point I was chuckling in time-honored gallows fashion because we were now officially into the "what can you do but laugh" zone. He didn't shut the whole session down outright but continued to peer doubtfully at the box. And then even more doubtfully at the valuation on the customs document. "Art," he said, shaking his head mournfully.

Well, the good news was that we didn't look like we had much

to hide apart from our incompetence. No one would value a silver box in the hundreds of thousands (just the box—no music)
unless they were insane or part of the art world. In the customs
world, you tended to undervalue items rather than affix huge
sums to bubble-wrapped hand luggage, and I think it worked in
our favor. I didn't look dishonest. Just stupid.

There was an opportunity for some bonding here, though. I
guffawed away about how ridiculous it was that a CD case could
be worth so much, joined him in a chorus of "the world's gone
crazy," and basically sold the concept down river to join hands
in mutual disdain at the absurdity of art. Laughing at your own
shit does tend to be a hell of a lot more effective in life than dragging out the soapbox and getting all adamant.

"Can't we just X-ray it?" I ventured hopefully

"Hmmmm." He stroked his chin thoughtfully.

And to my astonishment, he agreed. We had movement. One
simple X-ray later, he held me with his gimlet eye. "I should
really seize this, but I'm going to let you walk out of here with
it on the condition you file new paperwork tomorrow that actually matches what you are declaring. And if it isn't filed by tomorrow night, we know where to find you."

Who says that American border control is needlessly hostile?
Probably Cilvaringz at that precise moment, I'd imagine, but for
my money, I was ready to marry this guy on the spot.

I wrapped everything back up as quickly as my chubby little
fingers could manage and scuttled off toward the double doors
of freedom. Moments later Cilvaringz emerged, too, tired but tri-
umphant. Something about a clerical error on his visa. We were
back on track.

We clambered aboard a waiting SUV and bid the driver swiftly to Manhattan. As the fabled skyline hove into view, we breathed a mighty sigh of relief. That had been way too close for comfort on both counts. But clearly the universe was with us. Yes. The universe was with us.

We arrived at our hotel. We needed a debrief and I needed a stiff drink before we went our separate ways for the night. Animated chattering and uncorking of wines ensued as we called Gabriel and invited him over for a late dinner. Cilvaringz pottered around the luggage, unpacking and inspecting for damage after the customs shave while I kicked back in an armchair, sipped an inglorious Cabernet, and exhaled my cares. Bliss.

"Cyrus. Where's my laptop?"

DISARRAY

Panic stations. We shredded the suitcases searching for a glint of MacBook silver, but to no avail. The fucking thing wasn't there. I turned to Cilvaringz and asked what was on the damn thing, terrified that we might be in deeper shit than I'd first imagined. Apart from all the photos we had from the various shoots and the thirteen-minute sampler we were due to play at PS1, there was mercifully nothing, but we were now facing two rather substantial clusterfucks.

The least worst option would be the utter humiliation of turning up at PS1 with nothing but a box and a sheepish grin. If we were really lucky, the invites hadn't gone out yet and we might be able to cancel the event without too much of our shame playing out in the press. We could probably convince them to just do a talk and exhibit the box, but no one was going to be happy and there would doubtless be mutterings about how we were bound to do something like this and that's why we were mere parvenus on the art-world stage. Bloody musicians.

The nuclear option was the thirteen minutes of music leaking. I just kept thinking of the howls of derision aimed at government officials in the UK who had left laptops containing sensitive information on trains. Not only would we be skewered by all and sundry, we would see the album become a joke before our very eyes. Value would be wiped, credibility would be in tatters, and I imagine anyone partnering with us would have made a run for it. We would be a mildly amusing footnote in the history of hubris.

But where the fuck was it? Cilvaringz was eying me with thinly veiled suspicion.

"It was in the goddamn bag. You must have left it in the customs zone, you fucking idiot."

I excavated my memory with a bulldozer. I mean, it was possible I'd left it in the customs zone, but I didn't see how. I'd unpacked all the boxes onto a white table—the kind that didn't lend itself to camouflaging computers. And I had been so on edge throughout, so viscerally terrified of getting the box seized, that there was no way I could have just forgotten a computer there. And anyway, either Gary would have noticed or the customs officer himself would have. Customs had to be on high alert with the U.S. in such an advanced state of paranoia, and it seemed unthinkable that they would have let me walk out leaving something in there. I was pretty confident it wasn't me. So I turned the tables with a self-righteous screech.

"There's no way I left it at customs. You must have left it on the fucking plane."

It was his turn to glaze over as he searched his memory banks. He couldn't have done. We'd checked the floor before we left and he distinctly remembered having put it back in the bag. He had the mental picture on freeze frame.

"Was it encrypted?" I pleaded.

"Of course it was," Cilvaringz replied. "It was hidden in a bunch of baby photos and totally encrypted."

Small mercies and all. At least it wouldn't start autoplaying with a big flashing SECRET ALBUM sign as soon as some thieving fuck opened the lid.

Heaping blame at one another's doors wasn't going to get us anywhere. Wherever it was, we needed it back. There was no one in the world with access to the single copy, no one who could edit us up a fresh thirteen-minute sampler and fire it over. It would have taken flying to Morocco and back again to come up with a new one, and we didn't have that kind of time. Fuck, fuck, and double fuck.

To our immense relief, Virgin Atlantic actually had phone numbers in London and New York. There are few things more frustrating than being in a desperate panic, needing to get hold of your airline, and finding nothing more than an e-mail address and a ticket office that's open nine to five. Thank God there was a speck of customer service left in this world.

They swore blind that it couldn't have been left on the plane, vigorously protesting the honesty of their cleaning crews and explaining the oversight policy that didn't let cleaners off the plane without them being monitored for "items." It sounded mighty convincing, except for the fact that it really didn't, and unless managers were actively patting cleaners down, in an affront to their dignity, nothing would convince us that you couldn't get a MacBook down your pants.

We phoned Gary to see if he had any recollection of seeing it during the customs debacle. He didn't, but he phoned them to check. Zero.

Okay, this was really, really bad. We canceled dinner with Gabriel and began the disconsolate trek back to JFK.

The lost-and-found office turned up nothing, the customs zone turned up nothing, and the Virgin desks turned up nothing. There really wasn't much more to do than wait until the next morning, and as we booked a new hotel at the airport so we didn't have to keep trawling in and out of Manhattan, I considered putting my atheism on hold and praying like fuck.

The next day's opening salvo of hope was swiftly crushed by another tour of the lost-and-found. I was prowling the cafés checking people's laptops in an absurdly futile and rather creepy bid to be proactive, while Cilvaringz sat and rinsed through the options. There really weren't any. We were fucked.

As the clocks hit 2 p.m., we dialed London, wondering if there was any way the fucking thing had eluded the cleaners (the cleaners were taking a pasting here). It wasn't at Heathrow. It was gone. Fucked fucked fucked fucked.

One final tour of the possibilities at JFK yielded absolutely nothing, but by this point, we were pretty good pals with the guy in the lost-and-found office. We cultivated him with tips and kindness while stressing the importance of getting the computer back. It was a fine line between embedding us in his memory and making him wonder if he shouldn't take a look at the computer if he did find it. If we were this agitated, maybe the laptop was worth keeping?

There was literally nothing left to do but take a funereal ride back to Manhattan and find a suitable skyscraper to jump off. MoMA was the next day and RZA was due to get on a flight within minutes. We still hadn't told him what had happened, clinging to the hope that we could resurrect things without any embarrassing admissions. We climbed aboard the Misery Express and stuttered our way Manhattan-ward through obscene levels of gridlock. As soon as we got to the hotel, we'd start phoning people to break the news of a potentially fatal blow.

The descent into the Midtown Tunnel seemed a suitable metaphor for life as it stood that day. We emerged into the beginnings of a blizzard, checked our phones, and slumped back in the seats. Plodding into the hotel in a state of utter despondence, we limped toward the elevators and key-carded ourselves to the twenty-sixth floor. We headed to Cilvaringz's room, tried to open the door, and kept getting a stern red bleep in response. So we tried my room. The fucking key didn't work either.

"These are the times that try men's souls": Thomas Paine knew the score. Talk about getting kicked when you're down. Twenty-four hours ago we were preparing to be the toast of the town. Now even the hotel rooms we'd paid for were giving us the cold shoulder. Oh, how the mighty had fallen.

We headed back down to reception to get new key cards, and were just sighing in anguish at the gaggle of Japanese tourists in front of us when the phone rang. It was the guy at lost-and-found. A laptop fitting the description had surfaced.

Jumping back into an SUV to do the Midtown–JFK hike for the fourth time in 24 hours, we sped back toward our savior at three miles an hour. What the fuck was wrong with this town? How can New York have such dire transport links to its airport? No high-speed train—nothing. Aaaarrrrrgggggghhhhhhhh.

We were trying to tamp down the optimism and not get too carried away. We weren't home and dry yet. Arriving at JFK, we burst back into the terminal at a sprint, rounded corners with a dangerous skid, and thundered through the door of the lost and found. And there it was. THERE IT WAS.

We both had to sit down for a minute and savor the sweet, sweet taste of reprieve. But then the obvious question: Where the fuck had it been for the last twenty-four hours? This was way too long for it to have been found on the plane or in the customs office. And seeing as those were the only places it could possibly have been, what other explanation was there?

A rather unexpected one, as it turned out. It had apparently been handed in by security. They said that it had been left in the holding room Cilvaringz had holidayed in for three hours on arrival. But how? He hadn't ever taken his bag into the room, it had been sitting outside . . . Oh, wait a sec.

I had taken the suitcase from outside the room within thirty minutes of his entering. Was it possible that they had taken the laptop out of it to riffle through and then when they tried to put it back, the bag was already gone because I had grabbed it early? How was that possible, though? The pile of bags was in plain sight, and it stretched credulity to think that federal agents opened bags in full view of the immigration queue. And anyway—why not take the whole bag and check that?

We pressed the lost-and-found guy for more information, but he either didn't know or he wasn't saying. It was just too fucking weird. And you know, if we hadn't just gotten a phone call, we might have pondered the matter a little further. But we had just gotten a phone call. It was time to ditch the frying pan and head for the fire. RZA's flight from Los Angeles had been canceled.

Oh, this was bad. RZA not coming was roughly equivalent to not having the music. The event was in twenty-four hours, and with a six-hour flight on the cards, it was going to be touch and go for him to get a new flight out and make it in time. Invitations had now gone out to art collectors and the press and there was no question of delaying. Paddle8 swung into action, scanning the Internet for any hope of a flight that might make it in time. Alexander had been rousted out of bed, and a crisis meeting was in full swing.

Just when the cause looked well and truly lost—with not even a private jet available—a cancellation dropped from the heavens. RZA sped back to the airport, and we were back on. Heart failure was a beat away. Brooklyn, please, driver.

We rushed to Brooklyn to meet one of the world's most respected music critics, Sasha Frere-Jones, who had recently left a long residency at the *New Yorker* to join the website Genius as it expanded. The very same Genius that was co-owned by Ben Horowitz, the first person to publicly declare interest in the album.

Sasha worked closely with MoMA PS1, and they wanted him to moderate the discussion of the album after the listening. It was great to have someone with such impeccable credentials anchoring the debate, but we didn't want to walk into an ambush either, so it was vital that we meet up with him beforehand and get a sense of where he was. If he was skeptical, we would need to prepare ourselves for a more hostile set of questions, and to be honest, we really wanted him to hear the concept from our lips rather than from the press alone. So this meeting would be critical in determining the vibe of the discussion. We arrived in a snowy Brooklyn just in time to make our appointment with him.

We needn't have worried. Sasha was intrigued by the idea, and while he shared many of our own reservations with the project, it was clear that this was going to be an illuminating conversation rather than an adversarial grilling. Thank fuck for that.

He seemed like a really cool guy, too, and for the first time in what seemed like an eternity, the sun was piercing the fog.

The website catalog for the album had gone live that afternoon, alongside an exclusive interview with RZA and Cilvaringz hosted on the Paddle8 site. *Forbes* had a three-day lead on the contents of the interview, and their headline was of course the eighty-eight-year noncommercialization clause we had settled on in Tuscany, although we were disappointed to see it described as a "release date" in eighty-eight years rather than a commercial embargo. Then again, there may have been a certain naïveté on our part when formulating the eighty-eight-year concept, as it seemed to confuse rather than enhance understanding of the album and our reasons behind the clause, especially when filtered through the quills of some of the press. We felt that Zack had fucked us for a headline that suggested the Clan themselves would release the album in the distant future and an article that implied no one at all could hear the album in any form for eighty-eight years, something that would come back to haunt us.

It was supposed to work fourfold. First it would dissuade commercial buyers once and for all and nail the album down as a unique original rather than the key to the master copyright. Second, it would establish that this wouldn't be coming out through traditional channels in the minds of the public and give us a loophole our fictional hero could break if the album didn't sell. Third, its enhanced exclusivity would attract more rather than less interest. And fourth, in a world of headlines, you needed a number to hang the juice on—talking about copyrights and the mechanics of a single copy wouldn't cut the editorial mustard. A signature hook was needed.

RZA and Cilvaringz's comments in the interview *Forbes* wrote their story around had been clear.

RZA: *When you buy a painting or a sculpture, you are buying that piece rather than the right to replicate it. Owning a Picasso doesn't mean you can sell prints or reproductions, but that you are the sole owner of a unique original. And that's what* Once Upon a Time in Shaolin *is—it's a unique original rather than a master copy of an album.*

CILVARINGZ: *Initially we wanted the buyer to do whatever he wanted with it. But when we realized how much commercial interest there was, we began to understand that allowing it to play out in that way would undermine its trajectory as an art piece, even if no amount of replication could touch the original. We felt that retail commercialization and mass replication would dilute the status of the album as a one-off work of art and compromise the integrity of our statement. We thought long and hard about whether to defy art-world conventions and transfer all rights to public release to the buyer. But we genuinely felt that a swift public release after such a radical concept would neutralize the statement we are making. So we decided that the right to release the album would be transferred only after eighty-eight years have passed.*

And when asked, they had been clear that it could be released for free or exhibited at a price. The genie was out of the bottle, but we were far too swamped to monitor reactions. We had an exhibition to do.

BEHIND THE VEIL

Amid the sound and fury lies a simple truth. There is no idea, no artwork, no book, no film, no scientific breakthrough, no economic boom, and no spiritual calling that can touch human connection as the elixir of life.

Everything in this project that I had witnessed had been based on relationships, trust, and intuitively positive vibes, from my relationship with RZA and Cilvaringz, to the carte blanche given by Mr. S, to the friendship we had struck up with Gabriel. How was this going to roll with MoMA PS1, though? Would the sense of shared groove survive the exhibition phase?

We needn't have worried. The guys at PS1, Jenny, Alex, Allison, Rosey, Jim, and everyone else who we had contact with, were fabulous. I was worried about splits in their camp, whether some might resent our presence, and whether we would encounter any of that fashionista art-scene crap I was so allergic to, but from the moment the starting pistol fired, it was a team effort.

We headed straight up to PS1 after the meeting with Sasha. It was late in the evening, but there was much to discuss.

One of the primary motivations for PS1 was the mirror

image of ours. While we were looking to bring music to the attention of the art world, they were hoping to bring art to a new demographic of hip-hop fans. It was all about breaking barriers and cross-fertilizing worlds, and even on the limited level of thirty-six members of the public, that crossover was vital to us all. The question we now faced was how to ensure the fairest distribution of those tickets.

First come, first served was going to favor those living in Queens. Putting tickets up for sale on PS1's website would favor those who regularly checked it. How could we be as equitable as possible while injecting a bit of drama into the proceedings?

A plan began to formulate. *The Breakfast Club* on Power 105.1 and *Ebro in the Morning* on Hot 97 were the biggest hip-hop shows in the country, and both broadcast from New York. It was touch and go which one to partner with, but in the end, the consensus was Power, while making sure Ebro had an invite to the event so he could check out the music.

Through Angela Yee, one of the presenters, we got in touch with Joe De Angelis, the station's promotions director, and began cooking up an idea. The next morning, *The Breakfast Club* would announce that thirty-six winners would each get a free ticket to the listening; all they needed to do was tweet the hashtag #Shaolinpower and they would be in with a shot. The names would be picked at random when the show ended, and thirty-six people who were actually into hip-hop would be booked into the PS1 dome for that night. PS1 was kind enough to give the tickets away rather than charge for them, and by 10 a.m. we had a guest list nailed. Press, collectors, and hip-hop fans from New York. The karmic balance felt right.

Winging our way down to PS1 that morning amid the steaming grates and graying slush, we walked into a hive of activity. We pitched in immediately, helping the PS1 team move everything into position and design the dome's layout for the evening ahead. Lighting was coming together, speakers were tested, chairs were arranged in a semicircle within the sound field, and a projection screen was mounted above the stage. With the catalog of crises averted, it was time to have some fun planning the listening session, and it just felt so good to be working with motivated, creative people after so long in our own bubble.

Two hours before curtain, RZA finally arrived from his tortuous journey and instantly got involved, finding some black velvet for the box to rest on, finessing the spotlights, chatting to Jim about the acoustics, and injecting his unique vibe into the mounting sense of excitement.

I wondered if the PS1 guys had any preconceptions about hip-hop stars and whether they had expected RZA to swan in and start making demands with an entourage of "bitches" and gold-drenched hangers-on. Because it was one of my huge pleasures that day to see how he learned everyone's name, got stuck in, and balanced modesty with a creative touch that sealed the setup. It was as if the essence of the project was being played out in that setup phase, uniting music and art in a joint adventure full of new questions and new ideas.

As security began to arrive, bristling with electronic wands, we tested the music and RZA got behind the huge analog mixing desk to tweak the EQs and kiss the frequencies one last time. The thirteen minutes rang out through the dome, and while we knew that security could account for guests, we were uncomfortably aware that they couldn't account for everyone working there. What if the lighting guy was recording this? But you know, sometimes you just have to trust people, and it was actually a pleasure to do so. It would be what it would be, but we weren't going to insult the people helping us by getting them scanned. It was really, really special to just take a deep breath and trust.

Sasha Frere-Jones was nodding to the beats. It was the first sign that we were home free—here was an independent music critic of international renown and he was feeling it. Oh yes. We were on. It suddenly occurred to me that this was the first time I'd heard any of the album, too.

With the sound check complete, we repaired to the offices in the main building to prepare. The Paddle8 team had arrived, and we met Alexander Gilkes for the very first time—something that held additional poignancy for me because we had been at school together and he was still close with a lot of people I once knew.

It wasn't time for laughter and a good chin wag just yet, though. RZA and Cilvaringz were considering what they were going to say, Sasha was weighing up the angles he'd take, Alexander was writing his remarks, and I was hopping nervously from foot to foot offering suggestions and generally heightening the tension with my twitching. A vegan Thai takeaway arrived, and while RZA tucked in with an elegant gusto, Cilvaringz and I were far too tormented by nerves to eat. Security guards appeared alongside Tony, one of Cilvaringz's oldest friends from Holland and an absolute diamond of a guy. He was in charge of the box—the man with the white gloves and a trusted addition to the team. As everyone prepared for the spotlight, last minute fragments of philosophy wrestled for airtime with crackling walkie talkies as the guests filtered into the dome below. My gut tightened and I looked at Cilvaringz. He winked and cocked his head as if to say "Here we are. Let's do this."

The walkie-talkie staggered to life in a shitstorm of static. We were a go.

It was all rather surreal. Members of Middle Eastern royal families rubbing shoulders with brothers from the Bronx while representatives for Leonardo DiCaprio sipped water alongside a mystified press corps.

Jenny Schlenzka from MoMA PS1 introduced the evening before handing the reins over to Alexander Gilkes, who promptly defied the spirit and letter of the contract by announcing the album was on sale through Paddle8. You had to hand it to him— almost anyone else would have kept their trap shut and not risked rocking the PS1 boat. After all, he had decades ahead of him in the New York art scene, so tearing up the rulebook was never going to play in his long-term favor. Still, the enfants terrible of the gallery world had just met the enfant terrible of the auction world and decorum was out the window. You could see both points of view, of course, but none of us could resist a tip of the hat to Mr. Gilkes for kicking off an intensely formalized event with some brazen disobedience. RZA was chuckling away, whispering his amusement to Alexander as he retired from the stage, possibly forever. But Alexander did it with a cheeky, irrepressible charm and, according to *Rolling Stone* magazine, "in the booming voice of a London carnival barker who didn't already have us in a tent." Classic.

RZA and Cilvaringz both made introductory speeches and then suddenly, after all these years, the first haunting bars rang out. Raekwon's voice breathed menace and mystery into the arena. "Welcome. Time to shoot back down to the thirty-six chambers."

No one really knew the etiquette of listening to hip-hop in this kind of a setting, so the default position was best behavior. No cheering, no yelling, no "fuck yeahs," in case it proved wildly inappropriate. And beyond that, dancing or whooping would distract from the valuable seconds. If you were only ever going to hear something once, wouldn't you just close your eyes and focus? The blend of politesse and concentration distilled into a hushed anticipation.

One might question the buttoned-down nature of the seated format as defying the natural rhythms of hip-hop and forcing repressed hesitance onto the flow. But this wasn't just listening to a hip-hop record: people were hearing a piece of music that they might never hear again, and in some ways, it was a trip back to a time before recording technology even existed. The ease of access that meant you could cock half an ear to a track while updating your Twitter feed had been removed, so everyone in that room knew it was now or never.

So much emphasis is placed on memorializing experience with something tangible, whether it's buying a painting or taking selfies at a concert. But the best performances and the most electric experiences are ephemeral, where you're lost in the moment and having way too intense a time to try and document it. Those moments are truly transcendental, and trying to remember or define the specifics may be to misunderstand the nature of consciousness. Says the guy selling permanence for millions.

I think that for all of us, those thirteen minutes made one of the strongest points of the whole project. You had one chance to imbibe the music, and that fact alone changed the way you listened to it. Like everything else in this process, it was taken to an extreme, but the question lingering in the half-light was simple: What if we always devoted this much of our concentration and focus to experiencing a piece of music rather than just having it playing alongside sixteen other thought processes? In a conventional context, you know you have a recording, so you don't need to focus at that moment because there will always be another opportunity. But what if that reasoning rears every time you listen? Maybe you never devote your entire focus to hearing a song or an album? And that cocktail of transience and permanence was incredibly potent that snowy night in Queens.

The sampler ended on a funky brass high, and as a round of sedentary applause rang out and the conversation with Sasha began, you had to wonder what the reaction had been, as you simply couldn't tell through all the politeness. While the discussion unfolded, I snatched whispers of feedback from my perch behind the mixing desk, and to my dam-busting relief, it was looking good.

The conversation ended with RZA hoping for a philanthropist to buy the album and give it away for free. Either that or Richard Branson blasting it into space. It was a great note to finish on, and as more polite applause smattered the arena, things started to relax and the dome became much more of a free-for-all. RZA posed for selfies with the competition winners and half the PS1 staff, Alexander Gilkes and I caught up on times old and new with an animated glee, Cilvaringz was chatting production techniques with Hot 97's Ebro, and everyone began to unwind in earnest. People finally began trickling out of the dome into the freezing cold night, and as the flashbulbs rippled, the vibes were unmistakable.

On Sasha's recommendation, we repaired to Marlow & Sons in Brooklyn for dinner—somewhere intimate where we could enjoy great food while maintaining a low profile. That dinner saw the first real bit of bonding between us and Paddle8 over the ginger cocktails, and we laughed uproariously together. We all knew that whatever tomorrow brought, tonight we were intensely alive.

I awoke the next day to Ebro's Hot 97 breakfast show just in time to hear him throw his full-throated support behind the album. A swift cup of coffee later and I barged into Cilvaringz's room to start the Google News onslaught. What had the press made of it?

I don't think it would have been possible for the reaction to be any better. Everyone from HipHopDX to the *Guardian* was positive about the music they'd heard. Sure, many expressed ongoing reservations about the concept, but that was a peripheral issue today. This was about the music, the artwork alone, and not one single writer had anything but respect for it. The consensus was that it did exactly what it had claimed all along—it was a return to the classic Wu sound, and it sounded gritty as fuck. *Rolling Stone* summed it up beautifully:

> Whether you entered the dome thinking the elaborate packaging—hand-carved nickel casing, 174-page annotated leather-bound book—and high price was brilliant art or high-concept hucksterism, all arguments screeched to a halt when hearing the music. Simply put, if the full, 128-minute *Once Upon a Time in Shaolin* is as solid as the 13 minutes heard Monday night, it could be the group's most popular album since 1997.

That meant a lot. Of course the jury was out on the high art vs. hucksterism debate—that would never be fully resolved—but setting all that aside and addressing the music alone, the album stood tall on its own merits. Thank fuck for that.

We spent the rest of the day digesting the impact of the listening session, sidetracked only by the chuckle factor of various news outlets reporting the JFK customs story, which had been briefly told onstage. Perhaps deemed in need of a few bells and whistles, the story in some quarters was now about the locked box creating a "security alert" and finally being scanned through the airport's "rarely used highest strength" system. Well, if it was the "rarely used, highest-strength" scanner then it was doing an impressive job of hiding in plain sight, because it looked like a normal airport X-ray machine to me. Right there in a line alongside all the other ones. Still, you had to love the press.

We went our separate ways that afternoon, RZA to L.A., Cilvaringz to Marrakech, and me to London. I checked into a hotel for the night and set about getting shitfaced with a couple of friends in a private moment of celebration. It was all looking so positive, so untouchably successful. And of course those are the moments never to let your guard down.

Method Man was on the warpath. Someone had asked him a question about the eighty-eight-year issue, misleadingly suggesting that the album couldn't come out publicly in any form for eighty-eight years, thanks to Zack's headline. Which was bullshit, of course; it could be played at listening sessions or given away for free. Only thing was, that's not how the interviewer presented it, and more to the point, no one from our camp had explained it to Meth.

He went fucking ballistic. And you had to see his point. He'd signed on with the original concept, but now there were all these new layers to it that seemed unnecessary and way too self-involved for his tastes. He didn't want to get caught in the backlash from the fans about the eighty-eight-year thing when he hadn't even been consulted, so he very naturally went on the offensive. No doubt seeing Cilvaringz as the architect of the new clause, he regrettably took things further, publicly dissing Cilvaringz, which of course added fuel to any number of fires. And once he got involved, the fans had a champion and the personal beefs revved up. All the nuances were instantly lost as the story went full-blown tabloid.

We were in damage limitation mode, with calls flying back and forth between London, L.A., and Marrakech, and while RZA tried to stem the flow from his Twitter account, Cilvaringz drew up a meme listing the main points of the eighty-eight-year concept and circulated it to key hip-hop press before the misunderstandings could spiral. It was incredibly frustrating, as all of the more broadsheet publications had understood the concept and presented it fairly. But now we were in a personal street fight with publications that just didn't give a shit about the concept—they had some controversy to exploit and they were trumpeting it with unconcealed glee.

In hindsight, it was a strategic blunder to highlight such a controversial addendum on the day we were playing the music. We had planned on holding the news cycle for two days, the first with the deeper interview RZA and Cilvaringz had given to Paddle8 where they discussed the eighty-eight years, and the second with the music. Only thing was, the ramifications of the eighty-eight-year clause needed more than a day to digest. The fallout needed at least a week, and in making the decision to drop that on the public, we muddied the waters for the music. Those rave reviews held the news cycle for a day, but rather than filtering through the bedrock into opinion pieces and a wider consciousness that this album was the genuine article, we lost it to a very pissed-off Method Man. It was one thing for the Clan to agree to leave the handling of the sale to RZA and Cilvaringz, but it was entirely another when they started taking flak for our decisions. It wasn't our finest hour, and when all's said and done, there's nothing to do but admit having bungled that aspect. Such a shame it overshadowed the music, and 'twas no small irony that our attempt to reattach value to musical experience had been so savagely undermined by the conceptual dressing. You live and learn.

HIGH TIDE

Once the furor began to subside, it was time to assess our balance sheet. On the outgoing side, we'd played our last major card. Any further moves would smack of desperation: Just how many more things can you announce before people start to wonder whether you'll ever get around to selling the fucking thing? Media interest could only wane with further water treading, and while publicity was only partially a goal in itself, if the waves weren't harnessed, we would end up with a debate that had moved on and an album sitting in a virtual window with limited passing traffic. In other words, we would have fuck-all.

The chips were littering the middle of the table and we'd gone all in. But on the income side of the accounts ledger, there was serious movement. There seemed to be at least five genuinely interested parties. Not all of them had made it to PS1, so listening sessions had to be set up. Mindful of context and theater, Paddle8 wasn't content with playing the music in a conference room, but wove atmosphere into the thirteen minutes, playing the sampler at a range of locations ranging from the penthouse at the Standard hotel, which overlooked Staten Island (Shaolin by any other name), to the vaults at Crozier Fine Arts. I think five people in total, once they had been fully vetted, were invited for private sessions to listen to the same thirteen minutes played at MoMA. In each case, Cilvaringz would upload the clip to a password-protected page on the Scluzay website following a go signal from Gabriel or Alexander, then remove it immediately afterward.

Nothing had leaked from MoMA and nothing leaked during these private sessions. If we failed on every other front, at least we'd managed to remain impregnable in the Age of the Inevitable Leak. Fewer and fewer naysayers were confidently predicting a pirate version "any day now," and it was heartening to widen the circle of trust without ruing the consequences. The guys at Paddle8 were quietly confident without wanting to get our hopes up on fumes alone, but by the final week of March, they were able to brief us that four potential offers could be on the table within weeks.

We all knew that any offer would be dependent on a forensic legal dissection of the rights and protections within the transfer. Any deal would be conditional on whether both parties could live with the legalities, so while a formal offer didn't mean we were home free, it was definitely a start. Sure enough, we did receive four tentative offers, almost all of which had ideas and reservations attached in equal measure. There was one billionaire who really wanted to buy it, but was extremely mindful of being perceived as a rich prick with money to burn and trophies to accumulate. From what we knew and from what Alexander assured us about him, he was actually one of the most humble, low-key guys around, and it was a very fair concern. He was prepared to pay handsomely, but wanted to consult both with us and his advisors about doing something public spirited with the album. There was talk of donating it, at least for a limited time, to the hip-hop collection at Cornell. I couldn't help but register my fascination at all these Ivy League colleges with hip-hop departments. Maybe music was viewed as art after all.

Right in the middle of early negotiations, another huge music story hit the headlines. It was the end of March. And Jay Z launched Tidal.

Within hours, the entire premise had been torn apart by the media. It was one of the most misjudged presentations I think I'd ever seen.

If you are going to take to the public stage to address the question of value in recorded music and fair remuneration for artists, then don't do it with the richest and most successful stars on the planet. It instantly came across as an extraordinarily un-self-aware violin playing for the 1 percent. It was faintly ridiculous seeing this band of megastars complaining about not being paid enough, and they signally failed to present a coherent front up on that stage. It looked like an unruly children's party.

The real tragedy was that shortly after the botched launch, Jay Z went to NYU and spoke from the heart about the state of the music business, but by that point the ship had sailed. If only he'd left his troupe of celebrities at home and given that same impassioned speech about where the music industry was headed and how Tidal could help restore value, perhaps using two or three incredibly talented but broke musicians who needed royalties to survive, it would have taken a very different tenor. If you want to tweak the collective conscience into paying more while highlighting the link between revenue and creative possibility, then do it with the victims, not the victors.

You can, of course, argue that we had done exactly the same. Huge hip-hop group sells album for millions for the greater good. HA. There were so many inviting angles from which to shoot our concept down, but somehow we made it through the media minefield with a far more tolerant and open reaction than the carnage heaped on Tidal. The problem of course is that it takes a big guy to do something new or no one will ever hear about it, so to some degree, manipulating celebrity was key to amplification. But Jay should have rolled the dice on himself rather than his all-star team and positioned both himself and Tidal as a voice for sustainability across all tiers of the industry. To this day I believe that's what he intended, but having made that first fatal mistake of presenting it as a 1 percent sob story, any other angles were drowned out by the deafening roar of infamy. Poor guy. You had to feel for him.

So there we were alongside U2 and Jay Z in trying to address distribution models and value over the course of that year, and while both of them had been shat on from a great height, we were still alive and kicking. Interesting how perception goes, but we weren't out of the woods yet. Not by a long shot.

The day we received our first offer was a profoundly special moment. It looked like vindication, it smelled like vindication, it tasted like vindication. Holy shit . . . it was vindication.

At least on some levels. It was a lowball, to be sure, but still, the game was on. One offer provoked another as Paddle8 wheeled and dealed behind the scenes, and by mid-April we were juggling four offers, all in the millions, and all seemingly okay with the noncommercialization conditions that came attached. All of them came with watertight nondisclosure agreements about identity and terms, so there's only so much I can legally say about any of them, but just as we were taking the offers under advisement, a final player popped up. He was a young guy with a checkered past and we didn't initially take his interest all that seriously, though Gabriel felt he had enough potential to make it worth organizing a final listening session. Within three days, a fifth offer was in. This was much more like it.

It was at this juncture that Gabriel announced he was leaving Paddle8. It was like losing an old and trusted friend. We'd come such a long way since that first, awkward conversation, and we trusted him on every conceivable level. While we'd worked with other people on the project within Paddle8, most notably Kate Brambilla and Sarah Goulet, Gabriel was the guy we could call at silly o'clock and have a heart-to-heart with. It wouldn't really have a negative effect on the project, as it was in rude health and Alexander's team were all fantastic, but we'd been through the mill together with Gabriel.

Shocked to hear the news, we reminisced over the highs and lows and those particularly amusing two weeks near the beginning where RZA had stayed out of negotiations until we felt solid with Paddle8. There had been this unspoken game of cat and mouse where Gabriel kept trying to get RZA on a call and we kept finding reasons to sidestep. He had wanted to get the nod from RZA to make 100 percent sure we weren't a pair of con artists, while we knew exactly what he was after but needed to establish a framework before RZA came in and sealed it. It was all a bit tense at the time, but fuck, it was funny in hindsight.

It was good timing if it had to happen, though, and as Gabriel headed off to Los Angeles to follow his dreams, Alexander stepped in as the closer and we began establishing a tighter relationship with him. We had developed such a good connection after the Marlow & Sons session following PS1 that the threads intertwined naturally and we had regular strategy chats about the five offers, the people behind them, what they were saying, what they weren't saying, and what his sense of them was. Luckily RZA was in New York shooting *Coco,* so he was able to meet some of the potential buyers.

The meetings were classic. Here you had some of the richest and most powerful people in the world, and yet between them, RZA and Alexander cooked up a gloriously thespian strategy to feel them out and knock them off their guard. Still can't resist a smile about it to this day. RZA would meet them at Soho House and as they sat down together, he would look straight at them with a piercing eye and say, "So you want to marry my daughter."

They had doubtless been expecting a dash of platitude, a sprinkle of pleasantries, and a drizzle of shop talk, but instead they walked into RZA's most intense stare. Honed through years of chess battles and sword-swinging standoffs, RZA's eyes could bore through steel when he brought the full Samurai Apocalypse. Always challenge your opponent's balance to see his mettle.

It was instructive. Each reacted differently, but all were jolted out of their comfort zones. Whether they brushed it off with an uncertain laugh or detailed exactly what they had planned for the wedding night, it was an intriguing window of insight into the kinds of characters we were dealing with. RZA and Alexander no doubt had a shit ton of fun screening the suitors, and I can only imagine that our power-list buyers went home smiling, too.

It was becoming ever more apparent that we were going to have to accept a bid in principle, then wade into the legal process. The danger was that with an entirely new legal structure to develop, if it foundered on irreconcilable rocks, the other bidders might have moved on in the interim. There's only so long you can string people along, and if after two months of legal wrangling the process collapsed and we had to go rushing back to our second-choice offer, we would be in a far weaker position.

It was a leap of faith, but we finally went with the last player to the table. He had an unassuming innocence about him, and said he genuinely wanted the album for inspiration. He was motivated to exhibit, which meant the album could have a public life in ceremonial surroundings, and his heartfelt insistence that he wanted to close his eyes and let the album guide him toward new horizons swung the deal, alongside a handsome offer in the millions. The offer was accepted on May 3. Third day of the fifth month. $3+5=8$ . . . In the year 2015. $2+0+1+5=8$.

"Claudius. Release the lions."

Enter the lawyers.

ADVERSARIAL

I don't know about you, but in my less self-aware moments, I've often fancied myself as a crusading defense lawyer. There is a reason why courtroom dramas are so prevalent on British and American television and in Hollywood, but so underrepresented in the cultural fabric of mainland Europe; the adversarial system. They play directly into the dualist nature of archetypal art—the eternal struggle between good and evil, with the law as a theater of war where the bullets are honeyed words and the uniforms are cut from an altogether richer cloth. But the principle remains much the same: the adversarial system casts defense and prosecution in the role of warriors, each with a mission to destroy the credibility of the other and sweep the zero-sum prize.

Anglo-American society is underpinned by the adversarial system, while in most of Europe, the inquisitorial system reigns. Truth is a relative concept in the adversarial system, where both prosecution and defense set out a one-sided case and leave it to the jury to pick a winner. By contrast, truth is at the center of the inquisitorial system, and the vast majority of cases are decided by judges rather than juries. Judges may well be as biased as juries when it comes to a verdict, but the institutional frame-work of the inquisitorial system holds objective truth rather than subjective competition at the heart of law.

The adversarial system would be critical to the album's legal framework. There were no absolutes, only what two opposing sides could agree on. And therein lay the system's strength. But its weaknesses ran deep. When a legal system doesn't require lawyers to tell the truth and sees justice as a gladiatorial battle, then that psychology leaks into other social spheres, most nota-bly business and the media. The media are agenda rather than truth driven, for the most part, and businesses are well within their rights to sell you their wares with techniques that would make Edward Bernays blush.

A business is responsible to its shareholders rather than the public good in the same way that a lawyer is responsible to his client's interests rather than the truth. And that inevitably leads to a winner-take-all mentality without the nuisance of con-science. Which in turn creates an environment for extraordi-narily unscrupulous behavior, something that would figure heavily in our story before long.

But there was no truth here, no right answer, just a negotiation with no precedent. We needed two poles pushing toward the center. If the buyer's lawyers were going to come heavy, we prob-ably wouldn't get very far, and if we stayed too precious, it would be game over, too. Everything would depend on flexibility and the search for solutions rather than concrete protections.

We jumped on a "big picture" call with the buyer and his lawyer Nicole. It was a friendly enough warm-up dance, but one issue was already looking worryingly like a catch-22.

Just because we swear faithfully that there is only one copy in the world doesn't make it so. Maybe this was all some elaborate practical joke where the album leaks thirty seconds after the sale, we go home with millions, and the fans come back onside now that they have the music and someone else paid the bills. The buyer needed protection—and by protection I mean compensatory damages in case of a leak that nullified his investment. Sounds reasonable enough, doesn't it?

Well, no, actually. Let's flip this. What if the buyer goes home with his new album, listens to it for a couple of months, and then by month three has started to regret spending millions on it? Cash flow is suddenly tight, and what he really wants is a refund. He ponders the matter and then suddenly remembers that he's entitled to compensatory damages if the album leaks. So he leaks it and sues us.

Hmmmm. Well, the good news was that the buyer had made clear that he was looking to make this happen rather than cheese-grating it into oblivion. It was a major sticking point, so we took the tactical decision to forget all about it and address some of the other issues in the interim. Issues like exactly what "commercialization" meant in legal terms and exactly what he would and wouldn't be able to do with it. They wanted the noncommercialization clause to bend in their favor, which would mean us specifying all the things he couldn't do, so if he could think far enough outside the box to come up with a new method of commercialization we hadn't thought of, he would have options. We wanted to specify the things he was allowed to do, so anything that fell outside those parameters would be proscribed and we could sleep easy.

It was all negotiable—there were some questions about copyright ownership, and a surprising demand for proof that we actually had the right to sell this album. They wanted to see release forms from all the artists. It was the last question we expected, what with the album having been camped in the media spotlight for over a year and no one, not even an irate Method Man, denying that the album was what it said it was. It was food for thought. That and the ongoing sword of Damocles—find a way to protect the buyer against a leak or watch the deal disintegrate. It wasn't just this buyer, either; this was going to need resolving no matter who bought it.

In a wry twist, it dawned on us that what we were looking for was the Holy Grail of the music industry. Ironclad piracy protection. Wiser men than us had tried and miserably failed, but it was time to get our geek on and ransack the Internet for the latest technology.

It boiled down to identification. How would we know whether the leaked files had come from the disc handed over at sale or from somewhere else? Tracing a leak to an IP address would be a fool's errand, so attention quickly turned to digital watermarking.

Digital watermarking revolves around the embedding of an audio algorithm into musical files. A high-frequency sound is added to the music, inaudible to the human ear but legible to a computer. The idea being that you can tell which algorithm was put in which track at what point, so if the files did leak, you knew where the problem lay, even if you couldn't prevent the actual leak. It seemed like a very promising solution—we'd all go to a studio together as we closed the deal and in front of buyer, seller, and witnesses, watermark the audio and leave it with the buyer. If there was a leak with the watermark, we sued him. If there was a leak without the watermark, he sued us.

It was all looking very rosy until Cilvaringz shot down the logic in a two-pronged assault. One—the incentive to remove a watermark in normal circumstances was not getting sued for copyright infringement—and those that were most active in large scale piracy lived outside the reach of US law anyway. There would be millions at stake here and just one album to crack, so if you spent $200,000 on a crew of hackers reverse-engineering the algorithm, it would still be worth it. It might take months and cost a fortune, but the profits would way outstrip the investment. Immediately it was a different ball game from most watermarking cases. And then you had the other problem. The algorithm might be secure now, but what about in a year, in three years, in five years? We would be betting tomorrow's lawsuit on today's technology.

Back to the drawing board we went. Albeit slowly, because suddenly the other side was beginning to really drag its feet. Something about the buyer taking over a new company. As the weeks hobbled by, we tried to anticipate the questions before they finally came, so we turned our attention toward a solution to the problem of the release forms.

In a rakish tip of the hat to the absurd, the buyer wanted to see release forms from all the performing artists to prove we had the right to sell the album and that the producers had full ownership. Problem was, the release forms were covered by confidentiality agreements, and the second we showed them to the buyer (or indeed anyone), we would no longer have the right to sell the album, as by breaking the confidentiality on the artist contracts, we were rendering them null and void.

From Nicole's law office in New York, this was both completely understandable and disconcertingly convenient. How very cozy for us that we couldn't prove jack shit without risking her client's investment. This could have been a deal breaker, but in the spirit of cooperation, she finally agreed to take a template of each contract without any financial or personal information. It did seem fair—again, this album had played out in the full glare of the media, and anyway, our starting point for the whole legal negotiation was that we would indemnify the buyer against all third-party claims. So if there was a contractual issue, it would be Cilvaringz and RZA rather than the buyer who got sued.

There was also movement through May and June on the issue of what commercialization meant. We had to give as well as take, and this was one that we felt it was only fair to give ground on. We tried to pin down everything we could think of that he couldn't do with the album and left it at that. And quite frankly, if he could find a way out of that straitjacket, all credit to him. Any other form of commercialization would have to be so imaginative it would be a work of art in itself.

Paddle8 had brought in its counsel, Michael McCullough, who was an expert in the art market, but from our side, Cilvaringz and I were representing. Usually, you hire a lawyer because you are doing a deal that falls into a particular area of expertise. As a layman, you have no idea of the convoluted complexities of precedent that may lie within, but that really didn't apply here. This wasn't about seeing where the deal fit in existing codification; this was the art of the possible.

We finally got a contract suggestion from Nicole and set about rewriting it in a way that drew more on common sense than any reference to legal textbooks. It was sublime sitting in Marrakech's Café Extrablatt, hammering out a new legal framework for the world's most expensive album. Two panini and a side of legal history, please.

You got the feeling that Nicole was way more concerned about the small print than her client. You sensed she'd been instructed to just get the deal done unless there was a gaping hole in the middle of it, but her every instinct needed to firm up a very improvised deal. But she was never adversarial. She put probing questions and leveraged concessions for sure, but it all felt like we were working toward a deal that would stand a kick of its tires rather than trying to derail it with unreasonable demands. I started to develop a fondness for her, and it really did feel like we were on the same team—not because she went easy at any point, but because all her redlining was critical to make the deal solid. Ending up liking the opposing lawyer in a multimillion-dollar negotiation—who the fuck knew? But the protections question still loomed large. It could scupper the deal at any point, and we were dancing our way through the easier points of contention, desperately trying not to address the massive fucking elephant that sat in the middle of the room.

Meanwhile, in a Swedish forest, some seriously cool shit was afoot. There had been a couple of important elements to our concept: the sense of pilgrimage and investment in a piece of music. Not financial investment, necessarily—just having to go out of your way to hear it made it more of an "event." And the idea of artists being able to have a say in how their music is experienced. Well, these guys took things next level. Geospecifics, motherfucker.

A band called John Moose had released an album that told the story of a man, John Moose, who cuts himself off from the trappings and travesties of modern society and moves to the forest to start a newly arboreal life as a hermit. He signally fails to be adopted by monkeys or become one with the spirits but basically becomes a metaphor for the society he had fled, imposing owner-ship and exploitation on nature, ratcheting up his psychosis, and eventually having a full-blown breakdown and lying down, a broken man, palliated by the very earth he sought to control.

The band realized that since the music was so fundamentally tied to the forest landscape, the only way to experience it as it was intended was to go to an actual forest. But here comes the uncomfortable psychological twist. If you just told people to go to a forest because they'd enjoy it more, you can bet that hardly anyone would actually bother. Nice idea, we'd think, while put-ting a packaged meal in the microwave. But how about if you *forced* people to experience the music in the way it was intended? Was that just too up your own ass, or would people actually thank you for the hijacking of their free will?

The band gambled on the latter. They released the album through a GPS-controlled app that only allowed the music to play when the GPS registered that the device was in a forest. Fucking genius. Now that's site-specific art. They would demand a pilgrimage to a forest, and they would create the ultimate im-mersive experience under its canopy. Fuck music videos—this was three-dimensional lucidity, with sights, sounds, smells, and tactile triggers that transported the listener into the exact dream-scape the band had composed their music for. It was one of the best ideas we'd heard on this trip.

Over in the Valley of the Streamers, Tidal continued to hemor-rhage while a new player dusted off its armor and rode down from the crest of the mountain. Straight Outta Cupertino—crazy motherfucker named iTunes.

When Apple bought Beats Electronics, two things happened. Dr. Dre became the first hip-hop billionaire, which in itself was a seminal moment. And Apple showed its hand on an impending move. No doubt they'd eventually try something typically controlling, like producing headphones that self-destruct within fifty yards of an Android phone, but in the meantime, you could sense a play for the streaming market. With the dominance of iTunes in downloads, you had to wonder what took them so fucking long, but it was clear that the streaming technology rather than the headphones had been the jewel in the crown. Apple was making its move.

They nearly fucked it as badly as Tidal. Rolling out features like curated radio, to interest and applause, Apple's greatest advantage was its existing market and ferocious brand loyalty. From iPhones to iTunes, it could almost make up the ground lost to Spotify with its established customer base. And you could absolutely see the logic over at Apple HQ when they decided that it was perfectly reasonable to not pay royalties during the three-month trial period they were offering to subscribers. They were thinking to themselves, Well, if we aren't making any money, then it doesn't make sense to pay the artists—they'll understand.

Most artists by this stage were pretty punch-drunk with infinitesimal streaming royalties and poised to buy into the pernicious fiction of exposure as currency. We all know about the restaurants, bars, and clubs that ask musicians to play for "exposure" rather than something they can pay their rent with. The same restaurants which wouldn't dream of sending their chef to cook at your dinner party for "exposure." In Apple's case, labels and musicians weren't at all keen to remove themselves from the Apple catalog, as it was the biggest player in so many arenas and you wouldn't bet against it gaining the ascendancy over Spotify. Three months of fractional royalties lost to get in on the ground floor of the Apple streaming service seemed like a small price to pay.

The best-laid plans, eh? This one hit a brick wall in the elegant shape of Taylor Swift. She had already proved her resolve by pulling music from Spotify in protest over low royalties, and we couldn't fail but notice an echo of our own sentiments in her statement.

> Music is art, and art is important and rare. Important, rare things are valuable. Valuable things should be paid for. It's my opinion that music should not be free, and my prediction is that individual artists and their labels will someday decide what an album's price point is. I hope they don't underestimate themselves or undervalue their art.

Six months on from the Spotify row, she was the artist who broke from the pack when Apple announced that the three-month trial period would be royalty free. Surely the financial consequences of Apple's decision should be born internally rather than passed onto artists? Especially when it's one of the world's most profitable companies?

If I open a new bar by giving away free drinks for a week, then I don't expect my alcohol suppliers to gift me case after case of spirits. The loss leader of trialing a new venture has to factor in its own financial consequences rather than say, "Okay, guys, we're trying something new, so load us up for free." It doesn't stack up.

Taylor Swift immediately pulled her album from Apple Music and went public with her dismay. Intelligently framing the discussion around the young songwriter who just got his or her first cut and thought that the royalties from that would get them out of debt, she sidestepped the morass that Tidal had been embroiled in and made a universal point about the economics of music and basic business fair play. And with an agility generally unknown in huge corporations, Apple reversed its policy within a matter of hours.

It was so slick that you wondered whether it had been an elaborate PR stunt to make Apple look human. By changing their minds publicly in response to Taylor, Apple probably did itself more good than if it had paid royalties all along, but whatever the truth, Taylor Swift had again brought the issue of value kicking and screaming back into the spotlight.

REVELATIONS

July passed in a flurry of detail and redlines. We had no contact whatsoever with the buyer during this period; the only time we'd spoken to him had been on that very first call with his lawyers. We had, of course, done our research, and while it didn't look like he'd be winning the Nobel Peace Prize anytime soon, there didn't seem to be too much of concern in his background. Sure, he was being sued, but this was America. If you're rich in America and someone isn't trying to sue you, that's when you smell a rat. And he'd been investigated, but again, that didn't seem unduly worrisome. He was making all the right noises.

The contract wrangling continued. We'd always planned on retaining the full copyright to the album and handing over the sole copy alone. If he wasn't planning to breach the noncommercialization clause, then what did he need with the copyright anyway? But Nicole raised the equally valid point that if we weren't going to breach our obligations, either, then what did we need with it? It was too much control for either party to retain after the sale, so we went with the Solomon approach and cleaved it in half. More details followed, and disputes over exact language continued, until we were approaching the end of August and we had to face up to the seemingly intractable problem of protections. Everything else was pretty well nailed.

And then we had an idea. If neither party could risk paying cash damages over a leak, then maybe there was something else that could be leveraged: the noncommercialization clause. How about if we were to lift the commercial embargo in case of a leak? Ultimately, if there was a leak, no one benefited. The concept would fall apart, and walking away with the cash wouldn't be remotely enough to glue Humpty Dumpty together again. The whole thing would suddenly feel rather silly, and if it was leaking beyond snatches of lyrics, then the public really should have the album in its entirety and the buyer should certainly have the right to monetize the album, as what he'd paid for had been tarnished.

So we set up a series of milestones. At a certain percentage of content leaked, he would have the right to retail commercialization. In other words, he could put the album out through traditional distribution channels but not be allowed to use the music in films, advertising, or video games. The next tier of percentage leaked would trigger full commercialization rights, including all licensing options. And if the whole thing leaked with clear proof we were responsible, then fair enough, we'd cough his money back up. That would mean we had either been lying about a single copy, or else we had leaked it ourselves. They would have to prove our collusion in the leak, which in itself might be tricky to enforce, but the beautiful thing about this contract was that it was turning into a formalized document of trust. There was no way to make it watertight, and at some point we were just going to have to trust one another. Taking deep breaths all around, we took the plunge.

The contract was finally signed on August 26, 2015. 2+6=8. August is the eighth month. That makes eighty-eight. The deal had been three months in the making. All that was left was for the buyer to wire half the money and we'd start moving toward a close.

With the deposit paid, we set a closing date for early October. The money was in escrow pending a full inspection of the audio and the package. Mindful of the fact that only two people in the world had heard the whole thing, we couldn't risk the buyer listening to the full two hours, then saying no thanks. So we hammered out a skipping scenario where he could listen to ten seconds in the beginning, middle, and end of each track to make sure the audio was all on there. We asked him if he wanted us to make a digital backup for importation in case the CDs got scratched in transit, but he wasn't having any of it. That seemed like madness, though—what if they got dropped at customs?—so we agreed on a protected dark net server to place the actual music on until we were safely within the United States. What a delicious irony that this whole project would culminate with a download. Contradictions. Fucking love 'em.

We needed time to get the box polished in New York and import the leather-bound lyric book, the big leather outer case, and the certificates of authenticity. Courtney Ercolino at Paddle8 was all over the logistics—from sourcing the finest silver polishers in New York to assembling the documentation for import. We fixed a date of October 8 to seal the deal and booked our flights to New York.

And then it happened. Wait, that *it* needs capitalization. And then IT happened.

I was still basking in the glow of success as I perused my

Facebook feed one sunny September afternoon, when I stumbled into a nest of furious outrage. Some hedge fund pharmaceutical guy had apparently just jacked up the price of an AIDS drug by 5,000 percent. And everyone I knew was up in arms at the injustice. I felt a sinking feeling in the pit of my stomach. Hedge fund. Pharmaceuticals. It couldn't be.

Why, yes, of course it could. Because our buyer was Martin Shkreli.

I haven't seen a story take light in quite such a gasoline-drenched way for a long time. I suddenly remembered that Martin and his lawyers had been dragging their feet a couple of months back because he had been financing a company takeover. It certainly all made sense now—this was the company he'd been buying, and he had just skyrocketed the price of Daraprim.

Daraprim wasn't actually an AIDS drug per se, but AIDS is always a hot-button media issue. A triumph for social attitudes, actually, as in the eighties no one seemed to give too much of a fuck what happened to AIDS victims, and here we were in a position where adding the word *AIDS* to a story actually made it emote further. Daraprim was an anti-toxoplasmosis drug, and while toxoplasmosis could be a dangerous parasite for an immune system destroyed by HIV, it was just as dangerous for a body weakened by any autoimmune disease.

All of which was beside the point. This looked like price gouging on steroids. In the immortal words of *The Wire*'s Clay Davis, this was some shameless shit. The story had come out via the *New York Times,* and instead of doing what most corporate profiteers do when an unwelcome light is shone on their business practices, Martin set about digging himself an even deeper hole.

There's an unwritten rule in crisis management: don't give the story a face. Instead of giving a comment to the *New York Times* from a "Turing Pharmaceuticals spokesman," Martin had signed his name to the quote and then, as the story erupted, he made the fatal mistake of going on every TV show that would have him. He clearly thought he was justified in the price hike, claiming that it wouldn't affect individual patients and that it would provide money for research, but no one, least of all me, could understand why a 5,000 percent increase was needed if that was indeed the case.

He did not acquit himself well on TV. His explanations were garbled and his body language prompted a chorus of derision. It didn't do him any favors that there were a couple of unfortunate photos out there and that he had a penchant for quoting rappers. Within hours, the media had its first label for him: Pharma Bro.

Jesus—if he was Pharma Bro now, what the fuck would happen when people found out he bought this fucking album? The mind boggled. And not in a good way.

This wasn't just calamitous—this was Calamity walking into a bar, sweet-talking Catastrophe, getting really drunk together, smoking some crack, punching Fiasco in the face, then going on a shooting spree while eating orphans and setting fire to kittens.

Predictably, all his media appearances just fueled the fire. Turing Pharmaceuticals wasn't the story, nope—Martin was the story. Meanwhile, Volkswagen had been caught with their fingers in the emissions jar, perpetrating a massive fraud on the world involving the faked emissions of eleven million cars, but there's only so far you can hate a logo. Even with the CEO resigning, Volkswagen never gave the story a face, and that amount of passion just wilts on inanimate objects like corporations.

Which is how corporations work in the way that they do. Their very facelessness abrogates the need for morality. Executives who are animal-loving, charity-giving, Little League–coaching, God-fearing family men allow themselves to collude in shocking practices because they have bought into the insidious architecture of amorality. It's numbers, it's statistics, it's my job, it's not my personal morality. Therefore I'm not a bad guy. Meanwhile, the public is presented with nothing more than a logo to project its fury onto and a bunch of gray suits that can barely be distinguished from one another. The corporation feeds individuals into a system and through that system, manages to divorce personal identity from behavior in the company's name. There are a lot fewer fundamentally evil people out there than we like to luridly imagine, and self-perpetuating systems geared toward the mechanics of profit need a lot more scrutiny. It's usually not the player. It's the game.

Martin had missed this memo and had gone on what looked like a one-man crusade to make sure people hated him rather than the more abstract specter of his company. The really bizarre thing was that he really didn't feel he'd done anything wrong—as far as he was concerned, people needed educating in the economics of drugs, and then they would understand. But they didn't, of course. His explanations were confusing, no one wanted to hear about how American health care should be more expensive, and there was no getting past the sheer scale of that price hike.

Within forty-eight hours, Hillary Clinton and Bernie Sanders had both sensed where the wind was blowing and made drug pricing a stalwart of their presidential campaigns. This was spiraling hard. And the media had a new name for Martin: the Most Hated Man in America. Catchy, eh?

In two short days, we had gone from the sweet smell of success to the sulfurous odor of being in bed with the Most Hated Man in America. Everyone I knew was holding Martin up as the poster boy for the evils of capitalism, and there was no way out. We were locked into a contract.

The project looked to be in tatters. Who would buy a single copy of an album for millions? I'll tell you who—Pharma Bro would. Forget that we had other buyers on the table, that wasn't even footnote material. No, this would be the ultimate proof of failure for our concept. Or would it?

Maybe this was the ultimate artistic statement. If we don't support musicians as a society and all contribute to its sustainability, then it will end up in the hands of the most ruthless capitalists out there. There was a certain poetry to it. This had been an experiment in social dynamics, after all, and experiments didn't have a right answer. Yes. The press would buy that on the day I miraculously became slim and attractive.

It was true, though. Who buys art, anyway? Everyone from arms dealers to hedge fund sharks bankrupting communities to oil executives poisoning the world. Mother Teresa didn't have a fucking art collection. Just because most of the superwealthy are better versed in keeping a low profile and handle controversy in a silkier fashion doesn't make them any less guilty than Martin.

Is the art market built on the backs of the disadvantaged, the swindled, and the dying? Well, yes, in many ways it probably is, and look at us making that point by selling our album to the devil himself. This was actually one of the most intriguing outcomes we could have had. A philanthropist giving the album away for free and donating millions to AIDS research to celebrate wasn't a symbol of how the world works. It would have been the exception that proved the rule.

Try telling that to the fans, though. What did taking an album away from them and putting it in the hands of Dr. Fucking Evil say about us? Highfalutin talk about the art market and the music world wouldn't overcome this in the eyes of the fans. It would be confirmation that the Wu had gone to the Dark Side.

Cilvaringz and RZA both took it a lot better than I did. Cilvaringz was following the minutiae of Martin's logic, and while he conceded that the way Martin was making the case had confused the issue, he was prepared to hear him out in person. He wasn't going to judge through a press filter; he wanted to come to his own conclusions through independent research. Lynch mobs weren't his thing—this needed a fact-based analysis.

RZA saw it differently again. If you put a product in a shop window and someone buys it, neither the shop nor the creator of the product is tied in any way to the morality of the buyer. And anyway, if Martin had been making some bad decisions and was mired in negativity, then the album would open a portal of positivity and hopefully make him change direction. Maybe the most troubled guy in the world needed the album more than anyone. RZA really is like that—it's no persona. He genuinely believes in the positive power of Wu-Tang music and always views it through the third eye.

I, on the other hand, was focused on how it would play. Reality is the first victim of media hype, and how it was in fact seemed almost irrelevant to how it would be perceived. Jesus—had I become a fucking spin doctor?

Funnily enough, Martin had given away more than a million dollars the week before, but obviously that had no part in this salacious narrative. This was a proper black-and-white story—no one was interested in shades of gray. Suddenly evil had a face. And we were standing next to it.

THE PALE MOONLIGHT

Have you ever danced with the devil in the pale moonlight? No, but we sold him a fucking album.

Deep breaths. Deep breaths. There was no getting out of it. Contracts were signed, and Cilvaringz and RZA both had very valid points. We were running an experiment, Martin's personal morality shouldn't change anything, and it still wasn't clear where that morality actually lay beyond the prism of the press and his ill-advised commentary on Twitter. I should stop flapping wildly, settle the fuck down, and get a grip.

I didn't, of course. I love a good panic and carved out thousands of miles on my office floor, pacing from one end to the other inventing outlandish schemes to rescue victory from the jaws of defeat. I still liked the idea of presenting this as an allegory for the twenty-first century—it had all the requisite drama; that was for damn sure. When push came to shove, it was certainly more interesting than William Ambrose Samuel Partridge III buying it. It wasn't quite the end we had in mind, but then this was about discovering the album's fate rather than controlling it.

Cilvaringz was getting more excited by the day. Martin seemed like exactly the kind of contrarian adrenaline addict who might be persuaded to extend the life span of the project into an amended version of Tuscany's Plan B. Looking at the list of additional achievements playing Plan B could notch up, Cilvaringz grew increasingly reluctant to just call it quits with the sale. Having proved that Plan A had worked, he wasn't ready to pack up and go home. It would be up to Martin, but Cilvaringz's notoriously keen judgment sensed that Martin was exactly the kind of guy who'd be up for something this Machiavellian.

I was dead set against it. As far as I was concerned, we'd sold the album with integrity despite the identity of the buyer. Starting to muddy the waters with a limited-edition release and a bout of theater bordering on deception didn't sound like a particularly sensible plan to me. I could see some of the benefits if it worked, though I still worried about throwing the initial success of selling a single copy into doubt because of all the subterfuge that would follow. Breaking clauses, faking lawsuits—it all felt very messy and like a confusing distraction from a solid success. Let alone the sight of us collaborating with Martin on whatever level if it ever came out.

Only thing was that for Plan B to work, Martin would have to remain anonymous, as no one was going to be queuing up to buy the album from him after the Daraprim disaster, but if he could be persuaded to remain silent behind a different face, it could just be pulled off. It would need a Kobayashi-style character, someone to act as either the representative of the buyer or his partner, with Martin's name kept as far away from the stage as possible. Which was handy, because he actually wanted to remain anonymous. Announcing he'd bought the album wasn't going to do his Pharma Bro credentials any good.

Cilvaringz resolved to pull Martin aside for a private talk at the closing and see whether he was up for it. I insisted he not do it until the money had been received, just in case Martin saw this sudden desire to release the single-copy album as a betrayal of the concept he'd bought into. Couldn't have the deal collapse and him walk away with that kind of dirt on us. "Wu-Tang Lying About Single Copy, Says Most Hated Man in America." Just fucking imagine—the devil taking the moral high ground. OUCH.

We progressed toward closing, papers were received, and boxes were shipped. Tickets were booked and hotels reserved. I was in Paris on business for a week, and while I was away from Marrakech, Cilvaringz got invited to a dinner by friends to "meet our mate who's in the music business." Turned out that their mate was none other than Richard Russell, owner of XL Recordings.

Forged in the idealistic flame of early rave culture, XL Recordings had spearheaded a new sound for the warehouse generation, with sped-up breakbeats, piercing synths, tear-out bass lines, ethereal bleeps, and ragamuffin flavors all whipped together into a rampaging flow of revolution. Impudent samples and snatches of Jamaican sunshine flickered through Chicago house, uptempo funk, and hip-hop attitude. It was big-tent music, by the people, for the people, and reflected the spirit of unity and community that swept the UK. Black and white, rich and poor danced as one to a new musical hybrid that combined reference points from every creed and background from classical to reggae, unleashing new social fusions in the eye of a cultural storm.

Retaining its independence come hell or high water, XL went from the Prodigy to Adele, evolving its musical range, but never losing sight of the "realness" that was the cornerstone of its identity.

So when Cilvaringz found himself seated next to Richard through such a random twist of fate, the conversation swiftly turned to perspectives on the music industry, and it turned out that Richard had his own spin on the disposability of music. He had set up a brilliant project where he'd pressed a very limited edition of a collaborative album he'd done, but the copies weren't for sale. Rather than attach a cash value to the records, his distribution model was based on creative swaps. So the only way to get a copy would be to make something yourself and then swap it for the album. It was a genius idea, requiring time, thought, and emotional investment while also encouraging creativity and sparking ideas in people. It was the exact opposite of our concept, as the cash benchmark was replaced with imagination, and yet somehow the exact same themes were in play. When this was played out, we'd have to make something suitable to swap with him. That was for damn sure.

OCTO 8

"Looks like something out of Harry Potter," said the security guard at the gate.

Cilvaringz and I were back at Heathrow. And predictably, he'd been earmarked for extra security checks again. We were unwrapping leather-bound volumes, certificates, and paperwork at the final search and the mystery of this hallowed-looking book of spells was creating quite the stir as airport staff gathered around to check out our haul. With the green light issued, we boarded the plane and took to the skies, next stop—well, let's face it, the next stop for Cilvaringz was probably going to be his old stomping ground, the holding room at JFK.

Amazingly enough, it wasn't. He may still have merited extra security, but passport control was a breeze and we strolled out toward the customs area three hours ahead of the expected curve. Customs was absurdly simple, too—we had a good giggle with the officers about the exaggerated stories the press had printed about our last visit to their offices, and within about ten minutes, we were legal. The package was in. Code Blue.

The experience couldn't have been more different from our

previous attempt to enter the United States with locked boxes and keyless smiles, and we actually managed a reasonably early night. Just as well, really, because the following morning would be critical.

We had our instructions from Courtney at Paddle8 and set off bright and early to pick up the box from a restorer in Long Island City. Buried among the crumbling columns and ancient pottery that scattered shards of history across the room, our box greeted us with a silver flash of W. We hadn't seen it since March, when we left it in Paddle8's care, and the last remaining butterflies about what condition it might be in were put to bed with a cup of cocoa. It had never looked better. Stopping in at Paddle8 to say hi and iron out a schedule for the next forty-eight hours, we gathered our wits and headed to Michael McCullough's offices on the Avenue of the Americas to meet Nicole, confirm the final paperwork, and meet the man himself—Mr. M. Shkreli.

Cursing the crosstown traffic and the forty minutes it had taken to go three blocks, myself, Cilvaringz, and Tony, Cilvaringz's trusted confidant from Holland, ditched the cab and started walking through the Manhattan rush hour clutching the boxes. It was marvelously absurd traipsing around the city streets with our bubble-wrapped treasure, knowing full well that just dropping the packages, let alone having them stolen, would be an arrow through the eye.

Arriving at our destination, we were welcomed by Michael into his conference room, where Nicole and Courtney were poring over the importation documents for all the various elements of the album. It all looked terribly incongruous, this invaluable relic sitting there on a nondescript office table surrounded by white walls, with the packing tape fraying and the wrapping beginning to sag. We went over the final details of the sale and the last legal issues with Nicole, and then it was time. Nicole called Martin to let him know everything was locked down, and with his offices literally across the street, the door swung ajar just minutes later. There he was. The Most Hated Man in America.

We actually quite liked him. He came in with three other guys, and immediately the conference room began to feel rather overcrowded. It was small and functional, a wonderfully unpoctic venue in which to ink such a grand deal. Martin looked at us nervously, introduced himself, and for a moment, everyone wondered who would be the first to mention the issue at the forefront of all of our minds. I mean, how do you say, "Hey, nice to meet you. How's the whole Lucifer thing working out?"

I can't remember who first broke the tension, but it was with a risqué joke about his troubles. This wasn't going to work if we couldn't be honest with each other about the gargantuan clusterfuck that threatened to drown this whole concept in an orgy of recriminations. The first thing that put us at our ease was his willingness to laugh about his predicament, and the jokes kept rolling as he handed Sarah a business card, with the words "Just in case you need to get in touch with the most hated man in America." He was wiry, jerky, and prone to sharp movements, but essentially seemed like a nice guy who was hugely excited about the album, and not even remotely in a Pharma Bro kind of way. As we unwrapped the boxes for inspection, the atmosphere lightened and the tension ebbed away.

There it stood on the table, flickering in the fluorescent white light. Neatly slotted into one another like Russian dolls, the four boxes radiated a confident glow. The CDs were ready, and as Martin thumbed the lyrics book and remarked on the proximity of the bookbinder to his ancestral home, Cilvaringz loaded up the CDs on the rickety drive we'd bought in the Marrakech souk. It somehow seemed more fitting than a slick new one.

We were prepared for a tedious next hour as Martin skipped through ten seconds at the beginning, middle and end of each track. Cilvaringz had an inkling that he might forgo the listening, but I couldn't see how or why he'd want to do anything quite so cavalier. To my astonishment, Cilvaringz had called it. Martin listened to about thirty seconds of one track, rocked back and forth in his chair, smiled, and said, "Great."

And that, it seemed, was that. Inspection complete. He would transfer the rest of the money and we would meet back the next day—same time and place. There were just two things left to discuss. PMC had donated two speakers worth a combined total of fifty-five thousand dollars toward the project. The album had been mixed and mastered on them, and they were delighted to donate a pair to the eventual buyer so the listening experience could be "curated" in the intended spirit. We might not have a Swedish forest at our disposal, but with PMC's help, we could make sure the album lived forever in the sonic cast that sculpted it. The speakers had been customized with the Wu-Tang logo and had ONCE UPON A TIME IN SHAOLIN engraved into them. Only problem was, they were fucking enormous, and delivery was going to be a logistical challenge, as you couldn't just tuck them under your arm and stroll into a building. Martin didn't seem all that worried about the speakers, but he gave his home address to PMC so they could get on with delivering them.

We had to raise a final issue before we went our separate ways for the day, though. "So, Martin. What with you having a press profile that Osama bin Laden would have winced at, we're keeping your name out of this for now, right?" Or something more diplomatic than that.

He was very understanding, even going so far as to assure us that he totally sympathized if we had to criticize him in the press. He was under no illusions and hadn't retreated into a bunker mentality of "loyalty or death," as so many others under similar siege would have done. We didn't really want to start laying into him publicly though; we still hoped to find a way to get everyone out of this saga intact, but any hope of that would rely on letting the news die down and figuring out a reveal down the line. "We could do something like have a beef in the press where you guys are all anti–whatever I'm doing and RZA's calling me out and I can fight back and we can make it a real piece of theater," suggested Martin.

Cilvaringz perked up instantly. Martin was basically describing one of the phases in Plan B. If he had wavered before in his determination to pitch it to Martin after the sale, that sealed it. Damn, I thought to myself. I was mortally against Plan B, but any possible objection I might have been able to conjure was strangled at birth. Martin couldn't have been more perfect for it. Apart from the poisonous media profile, of course, but Cilvaringz loved a challenge. And you could see the glee as he wondered what kind of experiment it might be to see whether people would buy an album from the Antichrist if the stakes were once in a lifetime. How much do you want this music—enough to buy it from the devil? I sighed and resigned myself to playing defense.

We decamped to lunch at Parker & Quinn in Midtown, where the bartender Megan was one of life's special ones. And as we tucked into the seared tuna, it felt comforting to be back in a familiar haunt. Ilja Meefout, a photographer from Holland, had just arrived in Manhattan to hang with us and document the next forty-eight hours, and as Cilvaringz, Ilja, and Tony all caught up in Dutch, I wandered back to the hotel and got my head into a sea of e-mails.

October 8 dawned magnificently blue. Octo 8=88. Alexander had just flown in from San Francisco, RZA had landed from Los Angeles, and we prepared to meet at the Lamb's Club, a block or so away from Michael's office. There was only really one topic of discussion—when, how, and with whom do we announce the sale. Sarah and I had been bouncing a press release back and forth, but Paddle8 had significant concerns. They were about to announce a landmark funding round from the highest echelons of investment and weren't thrilled about the prospect of this story derailing that narrative. Their instinct was to wait a couple of months, let the Martin stuff die down, announce what they needed to for the long-term health of their company, and then put out the release with the buyer as anonymous. Announcing an anonymous buyer would inevitably trigger speculation about his identity, so even if we weren't going to mention Martin, sidestepping the identity discussion now would be a welcome relief.

RZA and Cilvaringz weren't in any hurry. They both found it hilarious that Flavorwire and *Vice* had published stories about the album not selling a week before and Uproxx had gone as far as a headline saying "Sorry, RZA, But Nobody Wants That $5 Million Wu-Tang Album." With the thing actually sold, we really didn't give too much of a fuck about when we announced, and we weren't overjoyed about the prospect of a Martin conversation either.

I wasn't sure that we could afford to wait. My fear was that within twenty-four hours of Martin's buying the album, a photo would be on Twitter of him with the box, and then we would have no control over the story whatsoever. At least if we announced and had the first few hours of the news cycle on our terms, we might be able to maneuver ourselves into a position of relative strength when the inevitable happened. Sarah, who was proving to be hugely astute, very creative, and a delight to work with, was torn between the two camps. She'd worked for months on the funding announcement and had Paddle8's future front and center, but she could absolutely see the need to own the story first if a leak was inevitable. I for one was convinced that social media would give the game away, and the fact that Martin had brought a crew to the inspection meant we didn't need to trust his restraint alone, but the discretion of everyone around him. I was sure it would take twenty-four hours for the news to get out and pushed for immediate release.

Cilvaringz hadn't told Paddle8 about Plan B. It was better for them that they didn't know, as they didn't need to be party to that level of conspiracy. But he was confident that by pitching Plan B to Martin, he could not only feel him out on his participation, but also guarantee his secrecy, as the leak of his name would scuttle the chance of a next phase. That would act as an incentive to keep quiet—silence for now on the promise of theater down the line. And more to the point . . . RZA didn't know Cilvaringz was quietly pitching Plan B to Martin.

RZA remained very relaxed about the prospect of Martin's name coming out. If asked, he would quite simply say, "We hope it inspires him to change direction." He valued Martin's rags-to-riches story and respected him as a self-made man. He saw something of his own journey in Martin, fully aware that as he himself struggled up from the streets, he had pulled some moves he wasn't proud of, and he wasn't prepared to judge someone else for pulling gangster shit. The parallel was clear; what Martin was doing had echoes of street hustlers trying to stay on top of the game. This particular jacking might be dressed in a suit and tie, but most other people who'd achieved that kind of wealth had left a trail of misery in their wake, too, just better camouflaged and more skillfully swerved. He didn't really care about the PR; it was more important to him that Martin genuinely wanted the album and had said the magic words back at their first meeting: "I want to let the album inspire me to do great things." RZA wasn't going to throw him under a bus if he was sincere about that—the press could take their best shot.

Sarah and I weren't convinced. Loved his principle, but we feared no one would get past the headline that Martin had bought the album. Truth would be lost in the scrum. But then RZA had played this game at the highest level a lot longer than any of us, and his longevity was founded on staying himself for twenty years, not bending at the first sign of trouble.

We left the Lamb's Club to walk over to Michael's offices. A hundred meters out of the door, Cilvaringz turned round and looked at me. "Where's the bag?" He had a set of boxes, Tony had another set of boxes, but the knapsack with the actual fucking album in it was nowhere to be seen. The knapsack that was my responsibility. Tony was off and running before I could even answer. My facial expression and the distinct lack of any baggage about my person did all the talking needed, and we stood rooted in a violently tense silence watching Tony run. I had just left a multimillion-dollar knapsack under a table in a fucking restaurant. I'm not a moron. Honest. Tony bust out of the restaurant waving the prize. Thank fuck for that.

We repaired to Michael's building for the final closing, but there was just one slight problem. Two slight problems, in fact. First, we needed a photo op, and while Michael's offices screamed discretion and professionalism, they didn't lend themselves to a magazine cover. And second, the final payment still hadn't arrived.

We arrived at Michael's office, where Cilvaringz promptly pulled Martin aside and gave him the full Plan B. I twitched nervously back in the conference room making small talk and panicking wildly that Martin would take the proposition badly. He didn't. He and Cilvaringz came back into the room a few minutes later looking like a pair of cats that had just staged a dramatic heist on a cream factory. Cilvaringz winked. Plan B was a go and discretion was assured. I put my head in my hands and despaired. Cilvaringz promised he would tell RZA, and on that basis, I agreed not to.

The final installment of the money still hadn't dropped, so we agreed to break and meet back later that afternoon, which conveniently gave us a window for a photo shoot. Alexander was all over it, and within a couple of phone calls, he had landed us the classic New York power view, forty-six floors above Central Park. Diving into SUVs with the packing tape fluttering in the breeze, we sped the boxes uptown toward the park. Ilja nailed the photos that would accompany the story and we all breathed a sigh of relief that we had managed to keep a respectable cosmetic face in the final innings. That was an appropriate backdrop if ever I saw one, and with the photos in the bag, it was time for lunch.

We needed somewhere low-key but stellar, and we were recommended a new Greek restaurant around the corner. Off we trotted with the array of boxes to Loi Estiatorio, run by the celebrated Greek chef Maria Loi. We had never heard of Maria Loi, but quickly fell under her spell. She took an instant shine to Alexander, not least because he seemed to speak fucking Greek. He was quite the boulevardier, it had to be said; in the short time I'd known him, I'd heard him speak Spanish, French, Arabic, and now Greek. This guy was really something.

The food was fabulous, and over at the bar, Kathleen Turner raised a glass to us. It was rather random seeing her enjoying a quiet lunch, not least because she and RZA had both been in *Californication,* so there was a shared history of wrongness there. Lunch was a joyous affair, with the table animated by adrenaline and fine dining and as we closed out the final branzinos, Alexander got a text message. The money had cleared. The sale was complete.

This called for champagne. Though with a Maria Loi twist, naturally. After we'd spent most of the lunch waxing lyrical about the magnificence of all things Greek, she emerged from the bar with a fabulous flourish, uncorking a bottle that none of us had ever seen before. I jokingly asked if the champagne was Greek. Silly question: of course it was Greek. None of the usual French suspects in this establishment—no indeed. We toasted the flawed triumph with a Hellenic vintage, and to this day I only have the highest praise for Greek champagne. The boxes had a chair to themselves at the head of the table and we wet their head gently with a drop. Goodbye, old friend, you served us well. Plied with desserts and good cheer—it was the perfect, bittersweet lunch to mark a monumental moment.

We hopped a ride back toward Michael's office for the handover, but crosstown traffic threw a wrench in the works once more, and as we cleared out on Fifth Avenue to walk back to Michael's, the unforgettable sight of Cilvaringz and RZA walking through New York together holding large silver boxes etched itself on my memory. It was both sublime and utterly ridiculous—it couldn't have been more obvious what they were carrying, but New Yorkers don't tend to look up from their reality tunnels all that often, so we executed a classic "hide in plain sight" operation and ambled merrily on.

For Cilvaringz it was a wave of pure redemption. All those years ago he'd walked these streets, tormented by the omnipresent W and losing all hope that he might ever meet RZA. Here they stood today, having just sealed a historic musical chapter together, brothers in arms as the towers beamed down and the gargoyles cracked indulgent smiles. They reminisced as they walked, and we dropped back to honor their moment. Once Upon a Time in Shaolin . . . dreams came true.

TO THE TEMPLE

The second I opened my eyes, I lurched for my laptop. Had it leaked? Had Martin gotten drunk and started tweeting wildly? Would today be an exercise in bailing water out of the boat before it sank? Was it going to be one of those days?

It seemed not. All was quiet on the Shkreli front, and in that second I had a new respect for him. Whatever anyone might say about his having bought the album for bragging rights—and the press would definitely say that—it was clear that there was a lot more going on than bombast. You could say one thing for damn sure about Martin: he was an interesting character. Good and bad are such simplistic terms and ultimately deeply dull— it's the shades of gray that speak to the human condition. It felt like Martin was incredibly smart, possibly too smart for his own good, and hadn't fully developed stable outlets for his fizzing mind. He wanted to do interesting shit and stir the pot in a morally dangerous zone. It felt like he was half genius and half naughty schoolboy, but whatever the truth, seeing the album finish in his hands was certainly going to be a fascinating ride.

Well that was a fucking relief. Fair play to him, he really could trust his crew to keep quiet about the album. The day took on a very different texture, and as far as I was concerned, we were on holiday and it was siesta time before our invite to Alexander Gilkes and his wife Misha Nonoo's place.

But before heading down to the Gilkes / Nonoo apartment for dinner, there was the question of Cilvaringz's meeting with Martin at five. I felt I should be there, not least because my mind boggled at what Cilvaringz and Martin might come up with, but for the first time in this whole process, it was made very clear that my presence wasn't welcome. Spluttering with indignation and convinced that my wet-towel approach to the flame of Plan B was essential, I protested in no uncertain terms until Cilvaringz pointed out the glaringly obvious. Apparently he didn't want a wet towel on his flame. Who knew?

We had argued every point of contention over the months, and the Plan B flashpoint was one that reared its head again and again. He knew my view all too well, and to be fair, he had given it every consideration from every possible angle. He just didn't agree with me. And knowing full well that my approach to Plan B was straight out of the Karen Gray playbook—kicking holes in every last fragment of it—he really didn't want me in the room raining all over his parade.

He went out at 4:30 to Martin's office with the sun high in the sky. At approximately 5:01, the clouds hurtled in from across the Hudson and visibility dwindled to a few meters. My commanding view from the hotel window was suddenly shrouded in an oblique mist, and by 5:10, a ferocious lightning storm was shooting down from the heavens as torrential rain lashed Manhattan. Jesus—what was going on in that meeting? Seriously, though, I couldn't help but be marked by the timing as an omen. The minute they began their meeting, Mother Nature began raining down Armageddon. I could only imagine what diabolical schemes were being hatched, and for once I was help- less to temper them.

Meanwhile, what seemed like a simple delivery process for the PMC speakers had turned into quite the drama. The speakers wouldn't fit into Martin's house—they really are enormous—so he'd diverted them to his office. Except you needed specific permits to deliver oversize goods to his office building, and of course no one was aware of that. The deliverymen had sat on the Avenue of the Americas for about seven hours accompanied by an increasingly frustrated fellow called Jordan, who worked for PMC in the States, and Dawn from PMC headquarters in the UK kept phoning to check on the evolving state of the plan. She was a total star, completely kept her cool about the fact that they had sent a fifty-five-thousand-dollar pair of speakers to a sidewalk in New York and no one seemed in any great hurry to claim them. In the end, the pressure of accepting the speakers proved just too much hassle for Martin, and he didn't care that much anyway. I remember him remarking that there didn't seem to be much difference between a five-thousand-dollar set of speakers and a fifty-five-thousand-dollar set of speakers, but when I suggested that the same might be said about the differ- ence between a hundred-dollar and a thousand-dollar bottle of wine, he took my point with a smile. But just as I'd be happy with a hundred-dollar bottle of wine, he was at peace with his audio setup. If he didn't want the speakers, though, I knew a couple of guys who did. RZA and Cilvaringz.

In the end Cilvaringz bowed out gracefully and wanted RZA to have them. They were something that money couldn't buy and with all the relics of Wu-Tang folklore RZA had at the Wu mansion in New Jersey, this would be an intensely special addition to his collection. RZA was delighted, so was PMC, and the speakers were finally delivered to RZA's home, where they would be lovingly guarded and forever cherished. It was a fitting end to the PMC story for everyone, I think, and a very tender moment seeing them go to RZA.

We headed down to Greenwich Village to Alexander and Misha's place. They lived in a duplex, a fabulously eclectic space anchored in bohemian grace. Playful flourishes and colonial accents brushed up against contemporary boldness and reassuring classicism, and as we stepped inside, it struck us that no stone had been left unturned in the hosting stakes. It was an intimate gathering of maybe twelve people, from billionaires to hoteliers to fashion gurus, and as the gin flowed and the wine overflowed, the flickering candlelight illuminated the laughter. It wasn't long before sombreros and English policemen's helmets entered the equation, and I realized that this was the first time RZA, Cilvaringz, and I had discussed the album socially with other people. Not for long, mind—we didn't bore the other guests senseless, it was just an interesting feeling to discuss it with such ease, safe in the knowledge that the deal was done.

It had been a fantastic night, but by around midnight, it was time to bid our farewells. Cilvaringz, RZA, Tony, Ilja, and I headed out into the street and regrouped on the sidewalk. I guessed it was going to be taxis home, but when I asked RZA if his driver was on standby or if he needed a cab, the look on his face said it all. He wasn't done yet.

So what should we do? Where should we go? No one was quite sure, and before the momentum dissolved, I suggested we find the nearest alcohol-serving establishment and take it from there. It's precisely that kind of blue sky thinking that makes me such a valued advisor.

All around us the night was alive. Traffic honking, ATMs popping, bulldozers rolling, and fluid grooves on the ruckus. We walked into the center of the Village, where the bars were rowdy and the whistles started ringing—"Yo RZA" . . . "Wu-Tang, Wu-Tang." RZA was always a gentleman and shook hands left and right, but we all needed a drink, except of course for Cilvaringz, who had been teetotal all his life. There was a sketchy-looking club right next to us—that'll do. They've got booze.

About the only person who hadn't recognized RZA on the street turned out to be the guy working the door. We weren't expecting VIP treatment or anything, but we weren't expecting a stern attitude, either, and the process of trying to get into this dive was proving harder than some palaces I've infiltrated. It was all on RZA, he insisted—he was taking his crew out, and as he paid all the entries en route to the bar, our eyes slowly adjusted. There was a live band jacking out some funk, but just as the vibe seemed like it had potential, they went into a series of wrist-slittingly dull R&B numbers. It wasn't really a cheek-to-cheek kinda crowd, they'd been a lot more solid on the funk tip, and by the time RZA pressed drinks into our hands, the atmosphere was starting to feel like a wild night at my grandmother's house.

It was perfect fuel for our groove, though. If we'd gone to a decent club, things might have taken a different turn, but here, the comedy kept presenting itself. The singer started trying to serenade what few ladies there were in the audience while his backing vocalist punctuated the Barry White bit with "Uhh-huuh" and " 'Cause that's the luurrrve." When he finally gave up trying to get laid and began walking round with a bucket, it was time to bounce. Thrusting a twenty his way because however Soul Glo he was, he was a struggling musician, we polished off our vodkas and headed back into the simmering Mardi Gras of the Village night.

We were back in RZA's old stomping ground and only a few hundred meters from University Place, where his office had once been—the end of the rainbow Cilvaringz had chased all those years ago. He didn't get to New York all that often now that he lived in L.A., let alone wandering around at one in the morning, and he was on top form, pointing out all his old haunts and bundling us into Mamoun's Falafel, where he ordered up a round of falafels and reminisced about his youth. Mamoun's had been there since 1971 and was a cultural institution in its own right. As the falafels fired out from the kitchen at breakneck speed, the vibe between us all was perfect. Fuck trendy clubs and bottles of Cristal. Fuck swanky after-hours parties and Meatpacking chic. We had us some falafels.

Exiting Mamoun's, we were waylaid by two magnificently drunk ladies, one of whom recognized RZA instantly and began selfieing him into submission while the other, apparently unaware that she was three feet from an Instagram post, earnestly gushed about destiny. It seemed that she had been due to go to London that weekend, but hadn't been able to for reasons too garbled to comprehend. What she did know, however, was that in the two words I'd said—"Hi" and "London," in reply to a question about my cute accent—she saw the hand of providence. "It was so special meeting you—it's turned it all around for me. You're from London and I was meant to be in London, and now I know the universe is sending me a signal that it's all good," she insisted as she gave me a big sloppy kiss and zigzagged off. Love moments like that.

It was all a bit too crowded now, though, and we needed a lock in somewhere. RZA was way ahead of us, and as we wandered down Bleecker, he was glued to his phone, checking out our options. With something seemingly resolved on the line, he turned to us with a confidential whisper and said, "Word—we're going to see my friend the monk. We're all good."

"Monk," eh? Was this some elaborate code? Was "Monk" some fabled producer or a fucking lunatic with a line on a mad shamanic potion? Was he the new-school Sugar Plum Fairy? Was this about to go all Velvet Underground? Maybe the Marsellus Wallace of the badlands? A subway sorcerer who ruled the tunnels?

Well as it turned out, it was even more fucking random than any of that good shit. We were heading to see a thirty-fourth-generation Shaolin monk. In a Shaolin temple. In downtown New York. Put that in your pipe and smoke it, Marsellus.

We arrived at a set of stairs that looked like they led to a warehouse party. Flying up them, we emerged from the half-light into an extraordinary space—part temple and part dojo. And the most extraordinary thing about it was that it was full of people at two in the morning.

From beat poets to ladyboy starlets, subculture after subculture has crystallized in the steaming grates of New York's soul. A catwalk of contemporary archetypes had long pulsated through Gotham—the freaks, the hustlers, the players, the fashionistas, the street philosophers, the B-boys, the gigolos, the tortured artists, the walking installations, the bondage queens, and the alchemical kings. All the gentrification in the fucking world couldn't strip that layer of magic out of the concrete, the fire escapes, the alleyways, and the perpetual night.

The melting pot we walked into was a truly beautiful thing. An enchantingly pretty girl telling the story of how her wedding to a gay guy had been derailed at the metal detector because he refused to take off his cock ring for the ceremony. A bespectacled kung fu fighter from Montenegro. A collection of chess-playing Chinese masters. A group of people you couldn't imagine in the same town, let alone the same temple in the middle of the fucking night. And at the center of it all, behind the speakers, was the magnetic figure of the monk. The Shaolin master.

With eyes that fused kindness and steel, Sifu was holding informal court. This was the family that had grown around the temple, from martial arts experts to chess players. No one knew RZA was going to visit; this was just how things flowed at the temple. You didn't come, practice, and leave; it was a community center. And a window into RZA's true self—everyone called him Bobby, no one wanted autographs—this was a home from home for him and you could feel him in his element.

Pictures of Tarantino in training lined the walls alongside a fearsome array of swords, and it got me thinking about the stylized representations of reality Quentin was so good at. RZA had always projected this image of a chess-playing, kung-fu-fighting, Eastern-wisdom-enlightened, mysterious motherfucker. And it was all fucking true. We were in a Shaolin temple and the chessboard was in the middle of the dojo. It didn't come any realer.

A lot of the guys were drinking shots, and to celebrate our arrival, the big guns were brought out. Initially taken aback by the presence of alcohol in the temple, I was schooled that during the Tang dynasty, Emperor Li Shimin decreed that the Shaolin alone among Buddhist monks could eat meat and drink alcohol. Well, this was fantastic news, and with the whiskey done in a flash, out came the most extraordinary bottle of forty-five-year-old Chinese spirits. Somewhere between a ceremonial ornament and a sacramental weapon, the fucking thing needed unlocking from its case with some serious Houdini shit involving gold and red bolts that looked like they had once held the Forbidden City together.

Hip-hop was pounding out of the speakers as the party came alive. You had guys abstaining from the alcohol and practicing kicks on a punching bag at one end of the dojo while RZA settled into a game of chess. It was like being at home, a truly incredible space nestled into the gloss of downtown. The music was sounding pretty fucking good by this point and I turned to Cilvaringz to say, "Are you hearing this? This is dope." He almost fell over laughing. "Don't you know what this is?" he asked. "This is *36 Chambers*."

Well, okay, I'd gone through this whole adventure without ever listening to a Wu-Tang album properly. But fuck, if you're going to listen to *36 Chambers* for the first time, sitting next to RZA drinking Shaolin moonshine in a New York temple has to be the way to do it. I was getting increasingly ebullient as the firewater slipped down, and before long, I was challenging RZA to a kung fu fight. I must have looked like Kung Fu Panda on the skids, with a burger habit and strung out on chili dogs, but I busted out a few comical moves while RZA held me off with an avuncular smile.

A few of the guys were jumping this traffic-cone-looking barrel thing in the corner, and never one to be left out, I signaled my intention to jump the living shit out of it. I'd show these kung fu motherfuckers how we overweight Brits do things, and I started to get myself in the zone with some over-the-top breathing exercises. Cilvaringz spotted the flaw in the plan—there was no fucking way this wouldn't end in tears. He pulled me to one side, put his hands on my shoulders, looked into my eyes, and said, "Do not do this. You will regret this. From the bottom of my sober heart to your drunken bravado, please do not do this."

Tish and pish, says I. Move aside, varlet. You scoundrel—how dare you impugn my athleticism. I was ten years younger and a hundred pounds lighter. I'd always been a sportsman. I could fucking take this. I paced back for my run-up, giving it the full Bruce Lee stare, and launched myself toward glory.

It didn't go well. It turned out that I in fact wasn't ten years younger or a hundred pounds lighter. Turned out I was just a fat fuck who'd believed his own hype and now my carriage had turned into an excruciatingly painful pumpkin.

Cilvaringz was doubled over in laughter at the sight of me sprawled on the floor—a fallen legend in my own mind. RZA had a big smile on his face. And Sifu was shaking his head at my abject technique. I wasn't going to cause a fuss, though. I've always hated it when someone lets the side down by doing something stupid and then bringing everyone around them down, too, so I just smiled through gritted teeth and tried to cling onto any last shreds of dignity. It was a tall order, emphasized by the way Sifu came and sat beside me as I clutched my swelling knee and put his leg behind his head.

We finally made it back to the hotel thanks to the anesthetic properties of that still-unidentified Chinese spirit, but I knew it was bad. I hadn't let my idiocy ruin anyone else's night, though; no wailing and begging for an ambulance like a fucking amateur. You break it, you own it. That's how it works in the intoxication big leagues.

I passed out back at the hotel and woke up completely fucked with a knee three times its normal size. I called Cilvaringz instantly and begged him to get me some crutches and the strongest painkillers a bribe of the pharmacist could buy, as fast as his unsympathetic laughter could carry him. He graciously arrived with the crutches within forty minutes, but it turned out that New York pharmacists were incorruptible. Instead of a pile of Vicodin, he had been palmed off with two-hundred-milligram ibuprofen pills. Which is just uncivilized.

Not as uncivilized as the U.S. health-care system, though. I needed an orthopedist, an MRI, and an X-ray. But I wasn't going to get any of them because I wasn't keen to take out the second mortgage I would need to go to the fucking emergency room. Back in "socialist" Europe, where health trumps money, I could have had all of the above for my taxes alone, but here in the Land of the Free and the Home of the Brave, going to a doctor was a guaranteed route to bankruptcy. With the HMO industry, the obscene billing practices, the backhanders from Big Pharma, the ludicrous specter of poor people voting against Obamacare because some rich fuck had convinced them it was a communist trap—no fucking wonder Martin was jacking his prices. U.S. health care was capitalism on crystal meth. Why the fuck shouldn't he join the party?

You always know it's been a good weekend when you're rolled out of a country in a wheelchair. A few connecting flights and a lot more medicinal alcohol later (I still didn't have a decent painkiller), I finally arrived back in Marrakech with my caregiver, Cilvaringz, who had been remarkably tolerant throughout the invalid phase. Met at the airport by my daughter Zara and my wife Madeline, who had actually hung up on me when I told her the news because she was so sick of my incessant dramas, I was somewhat disappointed by my family's lack of appropriate fawning. The second I was wheeled out of Arrivals clutching my crutches, Zara fell about laughing at the sight of her father's tragic undoing and didn't stop until we were at the car. Maybe I needed to rethink a couple of things. Like the present I'd gotten her.

I was going to be on crutches for a couple of months yet—I'd torn my ligaments, fractured my tibia, and fucked the cartilage. But hey, at least I could make a start on this book.

THE 8TH AMENDMENT

The primary focus of the next few days was to donate a hefty whack of the proceeds to charity. If ever a deal needed redemption through a charitable contribution, this was it, and our first thought was to find a charity devoted to toxoplasmosis, the disease the newly price-hiked Daraprim treated. It had a personal resonance for me, as I knew three people who would be directly affected by Martin's business strategies. Apart from the moral torment of knowing I had just been part of a deal with someone who was directly damaging the lives of my friends, it also seemed like the most fitting and appropriate way to offset the damage done. Except research didn't turn up any toxoplasmosis charities at all.

AIDS was consistently mentioned in the news reports surrounding Daraprim, but AIDS was only a part of the Daraprim story—toxoplasmosis afflicts people with all kinds of autoimmune-related diseases, including Lyme disease, and while fighting AIDS has always been an excellent cause, it is also well funded through the many wonderful organizations and individuals campaigning for research, education, and care. RZA and the rest of the Clan wanted to make sure that money made it into inner-city American communities, not only to give something back to the Clan's roots, but to make a positive impact in the lives of kids who just needed a nudge toward their own destinies.

In the end, the money went to a range of charities, from research into alternative cancer therapies, to the Children's Literacy Society, to creative programs for inner-city youth, to the Hip-Hop Chess Federation. Naturally we would have been on more solid ground if we'd donated to blue-chip charities that everyone had heard of, but that smelled more like image management than genuine gesture, so we went with our gut. Cilvaringz insisted on donating to TTAC, The Truth About Cancer, an independent team headed by Ty Bollinger, who had lost many family members to the disease and was now researching alternative cancer treatments away from the conventional trinity of chemotherapy, radiation, and surgery. Even though some doctors might queue up to criticize a contribution that went toward researching the effects of cannabis oil on cancer and others might paint a picture of us giving to a weed charity, we knew that the seven organizations we had chosen to receive a slice were honest, trustworthy, hardworking, and marginalized alongside global juggernauts like Oxfam and Greenpeace.

There was also no time to lose, because if and when we had to deal with the revelation of Martin's identity, the money had to already be in the hands of the recipients or it would look like some feeble rear-guard attempt to deflect criticism. By around October 20, the funds had been sent, and we could feel a little better about the sharp left turn our story had taken.

With all quiet on the media front and no sign of any leaks, I focused all my panic on Cilvaringz's determination to see through

Plan B. Every argument I threw at him seemed to bounce off his bunker mentality, and my confidence that a sudden epiphany would strike was diminishing by the day. His wife Clare felt exactly the same, and as we started a two-pronged pincer movement to talk him out of this insanity, relations hit a very rocky road as our joining of forces poured fuel on his most stubborn instincts. Problem was, people had tried to talk Cilvaringz out of so many ideas he'd had over the years, including the single-copy album, and with the doubters largely proved wrong for their lack of vision, the lesson he had internalized was to trust himself and not listen to others when he felt the end goal was worth it.

I tried reason, anger, guilt—the whole spectrum of psychological arm-twisting, to little avail. So far, we had sold an album to Martin, which in itself was damaging enough, but we still had a leg to stand on because the deal was done before the scandal burst. But anyone finding out someone from our side had gone into business with him *after* the price-gouging scandal in a scheme to trick the public that would involve selling copies of an album for a hundred dollars each would be Armageddon. With Martin in the picture, it wouldn't be an exclusive limited edition for a hundred dollars, it would be doing a fucking Daraprim with music, jacking the price 1,000 percent and selling the Most Hated Man in America the ability to exploit the Wu fans. It would be ugly, sleazy, and impossible to manage, and I kept trying to convince Cilvaringz that none of his goals would be acknowledged—just shat on from every orifice on earth.

He had fixated so hard on the achievements Plan B could rack up, and found someone who would actually do it with him. Except the terrain had changed beyond recognition. The fact that it was Martin didn't demand a strategy tweak, it demanded a

wholesale tearing up of battle plans. I could also totally empathize with not wanting this ride to end—there was so much more
we could do, so many ideas unfulfilled, and with the abuse Cilvaringz was taking from the fans already, he might not have
much of a future in hip-hop anyway. After seven years, the ob-
session was going rogue and threatening to swallow him whole.

To my undying, eternal relief, he finally came to terms with
the realities of the situation over the ensuing days. I sympathized
deeply, as I knew how much it meant to him to play out the other
phases, ones that might well have worked if we'd faked the sale
or the buyer hadn't been Martin Shkreli. It was like a grieving
process in many ways, and as November dawned, he began to
heal and accept that the second part of his plan was dead in the
water. But now that he had convinced Martin that they had an
alliance, the most useful thing he could do was leverage that to
try and keep a sense of where his head was at—to use the illusion of Plan B as a means to control him, if such a thing was
even possible.

We still had to announce the sale at some point, though none of
us was in any great hurry. RZA was about to launch an unreleased ODB song on a Boombotix speaker and was more than
happy to have the airwaves clear for that. Paddle8 was announcing a successful funding round and taking its whole business up
a notch, so it didn't need a toxic story muddying the waters. But
if for no other reason than to prove the album had sold, we did
need something out there. We settled on the first week of December and agreed on a statement from our side to go out to the
press.

I was still on crutches following my Shaolin heroics, and was hobbling through St. Pancras station in London with my mother, my daughter, and five fucking suitcases to board a Eurostar for Paris. God only knew why my mother needed that many suitcases, but deep breaths—it was all worth it for my daughter Zara to meet her great-grandmother.

About forty-five minutes into a futile search for Gare du Nord's luggage office my phone rang. Alexander Gilkes had been doing an interview with *Forbes* about Paddle8 and when asked off the record about the album, he'd said that it had been sold. He was positive that he had been off the record, but apparently the journalist didn't see it quite that way. She had told Zack Greenburg, and with his instincts on high alert, the news that the album had sold was about to go public.

An hour later, it broke, and unbelievably, I was still stuck in traffic somewhere by Gare du Nord looking for this godforsaken luggage office. The article was a rushed piece of copy and paste with cobbled-together old quotes and rehashed summaries, so our hand was being unexpectedly forced. Sarah from Paddle8 was also on the road (I hoped for her sake whatever she was doing was more productive than crawling around a train station at rush hour) but we agreed to send the release out so at least there was some information and quotes out there for other outlets to pick up and give the news context. God knows what the poor taxi driver made of the scene playing out in his cab as calls shouted their way across continents from his passenger seat.

Let's face facts—it wasn't the most exciting news story in the world at this point. The eighty-eight-year clause had alienated a lot of people anyway—it had been misreported and we should probably have explained it better—but it clearly hadn't got through that the buyer could tour the album to his heart's content, sell tickets to listening events, or give it away for free. The effect of the eighty-eight-year aspect had been to make the story almost irrelevant to fans, as it seemed like they were being excluded on purpose.

Follow that up with a story about the sale with both the price and the identity of the buyer still a secret, and the excitement was limited. The media reported it in a workmanlike fashion; it was all a bit "meh,": it didn't have any direct resonance to people's lives, nor did it contain anything remotely juicy. We'd sold the world's most expensive album to an anonymous guy and the public couldn't get their hands on it. Hardly an editor's wet dream. It still went global, of course, but without any real passion or verve. But it had to be noted that it was the twenty-fourth of November: 2+4 and then 1+1 for the eleventh month=8.

What was particularly fascinating was the dovetailing of that story with the phenomenal return of Adele. I've always loved Adele—I do wish she'd cheer up a bit in some of her songs, but as a person, a role model, and a star, I have nothing but the greatest admiration for her. The conventions of the entertainment industry are so transparently banal and yet everyone seems to follow them without question. Selfies, social media, lowest common denominators, tedious minutiae, an endless stream of self-involved drivel aimed at lowering fan IQs and keeping said star (or commodity) in the public eye at all costs. If you aren't doing your own Instagram version of *Keeping Up with the Kardashians,* then your manager will start threatening you with oblivion. Endless narcissistic bullshit of stars kissing parrots and gal-palling it up through faux-real filters. The best the business seemed to have was saturation as a PR strategy.

Adele didn't do any of that shit. Like a normal human being, when she didn't have anything to say, she didn't talk; she valued her private identity and had enough confidence in her music to let it speak for itself when she was ready. She didn't feel the need to cling onto publicity with the usual celebrity bollocks. And here she was with "Hello" through the roof, then releasing 25 to smash all sales records. There had been no marketing campaign. Apart from a few talk show appearances, it wasn't clear that any of the PR norms had been followed. And of course the public respected her all the more for it. You might call it an anti-marketing campaign and as in so many cases, ignoring the script and being yourself is the most effective strategy of all.

If I were a journalist, though, I would have looked at our story and compared it with what was happening with Adele. We had gone to extraordinary lengths with our concept because we felt the system was broken, and yet she was shattering sales records set in a time before The Great Digital Meteor just by putting an album out through regular channels. She was smart enough to sidestep streaming and its destructive psychology, though it's not clear how much that actually impacted sales. She had an incredibly wide demographic, but apart from her voice, everyone loved the voluptuous, naughty, cheeky piece of real woman that she was. And that made her unique—she was a solid three-dimensional person in a world of smoke and mirrors.

I remember hearing Grace Jones being interviewed on BBC Radio 4's *Today* program when the interviewer asked her if she would collaborate with Lady Gaga. You could see how the interviewer arrived at the question—you're weird, she's weird—but it couldn't have been more misjudged. The reply was categorical. "All these stars are too managed, too contrived. If there is one person I'd love to collaborate with, it would be Adele. She's real. She's an artist."

And that response from the living, breathing work of art that is Grace Jones said it all about the industry in so many ways. But Adele was the exception that proved the rule, and despite the joy I felt as she shattered sales records, you feared that not only was this not a renaissance, it was potentially dangerous, as people would consistently use her as an argument against those who said the music industry was in crisis. But then again, maybe with streaming off the table, actually buying an album from a respected and loved artist might rekindle people's motivation to do it more often. Who knew what long-term effect it would have, but Adele had certainly kicked the doors back off the debate. I hobbled down to the bar for accordions, red wine, and a good old French philosophical crisis.

BELIAL

This guy, man. He just kept doubling down. Now he was on camera being as smug as he could possibly manage, ruing the fact that he hadn't raised the price of Daraprim even further. From a psychological perspective, what was going on would have been fascinating if it didn't pose such dangers for us.

He reveled in jabbing up a mirror to capitalism. There was a cogent argument to be made that the more light he shone on the rapacious business practices in the pharmaceutical sector and beyond, the less regulators, lawmakers, and the public could ignore the vicious cycle of profit-driven health care that tears so many families apart. Hillary Clinton and Bernie Sanders had both incorporated Shkreli into their campaigns as a potent symbol of what they were against, and the House Oversight Committee on Capitol Hill was opening investigations on multiple fronts.

You had to wonder why Martin had chosen this kamikaze path of confrontation. There were some telling factors. He was clearly extremely clever on a number of levels and had felt alienated from a whole spectrum of establishments—from high school cliques to executive lounges. He had plunged down a maverick tunnel throughout his early business career, but I wondered if the scandal around Daraprim had flicked a switch that accelerated his trajectory onto a different plane entirely. I had a feeling that when he charged onto any TV network that would have him to discuss the Daraprim hike on that first fateful day in September, he thought that he was being provocative but essentially honest about the workings of capitalism; where regulation was left flapping in the wind by lawmakers awash in lobbyist money and corporate pressure. The rules allowed it, his shareholders demanded profits, and surely the American dream as warped by Reaganomics held the market as the ultimate arbiter of right and wrong.

But he'd miscalculated wildly. The rest of the corporate establishment needed to paint him as a renegade so as not to attract any unwelcome attention to their own business practices. Polished and discreet they might be, but when you boil it down, much of what Martin was actually doing was entrenched in the worldview of thousands of cutthroat companies. And the public finally had someone to fixate their anger and outrage on—a face, and a very punchable face at that. He was the perfect foil for an extraordinarily wide coalition.

The word *sociopath* was thrown around very liberally in the first flush of the Daraprim scandal, and naturally it was largely being used as a dramatic device by a sensationalist media to conjure the image of a heartless, soulless, almost inhuman villain. But it rang a bell for different reasons. A core element of sociopathy is the inability to properly empathize, a trait that results in a limited conscience, but what it also signifies is the inability to feel what others feel or predict how people might react to your behavior because you simply can't see it from their perspective.

I think he was genuinely surprised at the tsunami of contempt that washed over him, and it triggered a familiar sense of rejection. He couldn't understand why the world kept ostracizing him, and if still at this point in his life no one either could or indeed wanted to understand him, then fuck 'em all. He'd take this to the extreme. "The Most Evil Man in the World" might not have been a crown he sought, but now that the world had placed it on his head, he'd play up to it for everything he was worth. It's a theory.

Meanwhile, Bloomberg was doing an in-depth story on the sale of the album, and had spoken to all the players from the sale side. Cilvaringz had kept a line of communication open to Martin since realizing that Plan B was suicide, and all seemed fine. The anonymity question wasn't set to be reopened, as far as any of us knew, although an early alarm bell came when Martin said that he thought Bloomberg journalist Devin Leonard knew he was the buyer. We genuinely couldn't see how breaking anonymity might be desirable for Martin, as it would just be used as a stick to beat him and raise all kinds of questions about where the money he was making from sick children was actually going. The glaring hole in our logic was that we were using our own empathy to guess his motives, and he didn't think like most people. What made sense to us made no sense whatsoever to him. He didn't care about bad press. Quite the contrary—he was thirsting after it like a crackhead frantically trying to score his next rock.

There were a couple of other worrying signs in that first week of December, most notably when Martin called Cilvaringz and said that he'd gotten drunk and told a few girls that he owned the album. His conclusion was that the news would leak very soon, but that was quite a stretch. Telling a couple of girls doesn't mean headline news by a long shot. But if he was talking to

Bloomberg and using the girls' story as a feeble cover, then that would make far more sense. And Devin, playing his cards very close to his chest, asked us questions about who decided on the anonymity, and RZA sincerely responded that it had been a mutual decision. Devin said that he would talk to the buyer and see if the buyer felt the same. So he did know for sure that it was Martin, and while Martin had assured us that he wanted to remain anonymous at least for the time being, there was a decidedly strange wind blowing.

And then it happened. An e-mail from Devin giving us an hour to comment on three main elements: The identity of the buyer. The price. And something Alexander Gilkes had apparently said to Martin about how if he bought the album, "celebrities and rappers" would want to hang out with him.

Fuck—OK—well . . . If Martin wanted to go public with his name—then that was his right. The price thing was very odd, Bloomberg had attributed it to "a source close to the story" which basically meant Martin himself as it certainly hadn't come from any of us, and to this day we still haven't confirmed if it's the real price or not.

RZA fired over a quote that sought simply to make clear that the deal was agreed on well before we knew anything about Martin's business practices and that we'd given money to charity. He had about five minutes to do it in, too, because most of the hour Devin had given us was spent trying to get hold of RZA. RZA's statement didn't attack Martin personally or pass judgment—but people had to know that we didn't do this deal with the full knowledge of what he was up to, and they had to know that money had gone to good causes. It was the minimum.

But the Alexander quote. It was pure hearsay—and hearsay

from that bastion of truth Martin Shkreli. Alexander was really hurt at the suggestion that he went around promising fame by association but was forbidden by convention to comment on private conversations. We tried to have that quote taken out in solidarity with Alexander, and we were disappointed with Bloomberg for keeping it in when they had no corroboration of any sort. The quote was obviously left in to make Martin look as stupid as possible, because he went on to say that he had bought the album for that reason. Jesus. It was like this guy had an irresistible impulse to be hated.

The news broke to a predictable avalanche of outrage. This was a real story. Fuck that mealy-mouthed shit from a few weeks ago where the album sold for an undisclosed amount to an undisclosed buyer. That was yawn central. But THIS—now THIS was a story.

As the headlines cascaded, there was one thing that we heard that Martin had said that immediately pissed us off. That he hadn't listened to the album and might well never bother. A sentiment he compounded later on one of his bizarrely narcissistic live streams when he said he got more enjoyment out of keeping the album away from fans than from the music. That was fucking outrageous, especially as he had spun a load of bullshit about how he had wanted it to inspire him. And while the fact that this villain of pantomime proportions had the album was shocking enough, the idea that he didn't even care enough to listen to it was the ultimate kick in the balls. Thing was, by this stage we had enough of a sense of Martin's character to wonder if he'd said that because it was true, or because it was the most antagonistic thing he could possibly have come out with. My money would be on the latter, a hunch only fueled by Martin saying things like "Within ten years, more than half of all rap/ hip-hop music will be made exclusively for me. Don't worry—I will share some of it."

The real concern about the Martin reveal was not that people would think we went into the deal with eyes open, because even he had confirmed that the deal was done before the Daraprim dam burst. Would this be taken as conclusive proof that it had been a fucking stupid idea because who else but a braggadocio millionaire was going to buy this album? You didn't make that kind of money adopting orphans, and people might argue that you didn't buy rap albums at that price unless you were an ego-maniac. The *Atlantic* was the first to take that line, millions of fans were feeling exactly the same, and I desperately wanted our side to come out and say, THIS WAS THE ARTISTIC STATEMENT. It's a clear symbol of what will happen unless we support our artists as a society by paying them a fair price and respecting the music we love. If we don't, it will end up dis-torted beyond recognition by an elite few. Whether they be Martin Shkreli or Simon Cowell.

From the start, this album would chart its own course and let destiny shape its message. Whatever happened to it would be a mirror to our society, and while making ownership conditional on the size of someone's bank account was distasteful, it would never have come to that if everybody paid a fair amount for the music they listened to. It was both action and reaction, both provocation and backlash, and what was happening here really was an allegory for our times. But better, because even the most outlandish Hollywood scriptwriters would never have come up with such a pastiche bad guy.

No doubt, the general feeling out there in the world and the hip-hop community was that we all needed a shower. There was a certain sense of Martin laughing at the Clan and all the Wu fans, and the *New York Post* even went so far as to change the headline on their story two hours after launch to "Jackass Drug CEO Destroys a Rap Icon." If the public mood settled there, that somehow our elaborate plan had led to us being owned by this guy in a humiliating morass of shame, then that was going to be incredibly difficult to come back from.

The opinions and editorials would doubtless be more withering than the news reports, but we weren't there yet. Everyone was still digesting the enormity that of all the people in the world, Martin Shkreli had the secret Wu-Tang album.

Over on Twitter, there was an epic shitstorm in full flow, and both Wu-Tang Clan and Martin Shkreli were trending for hours on end. Two tweets stick in my mind most of all. One was from Congress—the Democrats on the House Oversight Committee had actually made a meme entitled "What 2 Million Buys You." It contained a huge Wu logo under the word *May.* Then, under *July,* they had a big bottle of Daraprim. And then finally they had a tiny bottle of Daraprim under *August* to reflect the price hike—and the size of the Wu logo against the tiny bottle of pills made its point rather effectively. Shit: Congress were doing memes including Wu logos. Could this get any stranger? You bet it could.

If I ever meet Rob Wesley of Philadelphia, I am going to kiss him and have his babies. Rob, if you're reading this, take cover, because I'm no oil painting. Rob had put an image on Twitter that looked deliciously realistic. It seemed to be an excerpt from the sales contract that referenced one specific clause. And here's what it said:

> The buying party also agrees that, at any time during
> the stipulated 88 year period, the seller may legally plan
> and attempt to execute one (1) heist or caper to steal
> back *Once Upon A Time In Shaolin,* which, if successful,
> would return all ownership rights to the seller. Said
> heist or caper can only be undertaken by currently
> active members of the Wu-Tang Clan and/or actor Bill
> Murray, with no legal repercussions.

It was fucking hilarious, and the choice of Bill Murray was truly inspired. He had a history with the Clan, having appeared in Jim Jarmusch's *Coffee and Cigarettes* alongside RZA and GZA, and he was also one of the most gloriously random dudes out there, with a history of wandering into odd scenarios like crashing parties to do the dishes and losing endless A-list roles because he had no agent or manager, just an 800 number and an answering machine. The image of the Wu-Tang Clan executing a heist with Bill Murray was pure surrealist magic.

As the retweets pushed past five thousand, it became increasingly clear that a lot of people actually believed it, and the suspension of disbelief that is such a key human component of great art was firing on all cylinders. No one stopped to ask how the hell this guy had access to the contract, and people shelved their critical faculties because they so wanted it to be true. No one wanted the story to end with the album in Martin's hands as he trolled the world. They wanted not only further drama, but a sense that good would prevail in the end. That somewhere, somehow, there might be a fairy tale ending.

Still, I couldn't believe it when UK national broadsheet the *Independent* reported it almost as fact. It beggared belief that they went in with such a categorical headline and some pretty minimal caveats in the article without comment or verification, but once they did, the dominos started to fall. And if they could do that with a hip-hop album, just think what happens with misinformation and disinformation about wars, politics, and the decisions that shape our lives.

More and more news outlets picked it up, and even those who were dubious about the clause's provenance just covered themselves with a few *reportedly*s and *allegedly*s to allow them to perpetuate the story. And why not? It was a gift from the heavens, a sublime addition to this unfolding tale, where even if it wasn't true, it was still too good not to print.

Recent years have seen the cannibalization of the press, where Internet hoaxes, rumors, memes, and tricks filter into the news cycle and established institutions trawl the Web for the most comical and bizarre stories out there. It has been a parallel process to what happened in the music industry—blogs and free online news led to saturation, a dilution of what constituted journalism, a savage new economic landscape, and the mass layoff of reporters who would dig out actual news. With competition increasingly desperate, huge swathes of the press began recycling content that they couldn't afford to source themselves, with clickbait headlines to ramp up the paltry pennies earned through advertising. Stories didn't need to be true anymore; just reporting that something was a big thing on the Net was enough to make an article worth writing. And most telling of all was that even the articles that exposed the Bill Murray hoax invariably finished with something along the lines of "wouldn't it be great if it were true" or "let's hope the Clan take inspiration from this."

Above all, the Bill Murray wild card had completely changed the tone. It went from sleazy and mournful to hopeful and hilarious. Such was the legacy of the Wu-Tang Clan that people actually believed such a clause could be in the contract—a profound testament in itself to the Clan. The story was suddenly inclusive and fun again. No longer was everyone cut out of the loop by an obstreperous millionaire; they were all part of a drama, a fight between good and evil, a dualist battle of wills involving Bill Murray and the most mysterious album of all time.

RZA instantly saw the humor in it and tweeted himself, "We're really feeling the urge to call Bill Murray," and that even made headlines after the hoax was exposed. When outlets like *Fortune* are running articles like "RZA Is Tempted to Steal Back $2 Million Wu-Tang Album from Martin Shkreli," you know that you've hit a perfect cultural storm. True, not true—who cares? This is fucking great.

And behind the scenes, we were having one conversation and one conversation alone, even as a guy named Jordan VanDina posted a seventy-page script online featuring a supporting cast of Kim Jong-Un, Justin Bieber, and ODB's ghost. Should we turn fiction into truth? Shall we harness this moment and make it happen? Who had Bill Murray's 800 number? And how could we play this? It felt like the album was writing another chapter for itself with the help of Rob Wesley Esquire, the world's press, and the social media zeitgeist. However ridiculous the hand we'd been dealt looked, we owed it to the universe to throw in our chips and gamble.

COFFEE AND SKI MASKS

All eyes turned to our Plotter in Chief. If you ever need a fiendishly cunning plan that is dripping with theatrics, laced with intrigue, blurs the lines between plausibility and madness, and fuses a fascinating outcome with a devilish twist of mischief, then Mr. Tarik "Cilvaringz" Azzougarh is your man. I just kept thanking my lucky fucking stars that we were on the same side.

Cilvaringz hadn't been able to get hold of Martin since the Bloomberg article took the reveal of his identity nuclear. As far as Martin was concerned, a Plan B where he loopholed the noncommercialization clause was still on the table, but he was doubtless ducking calls to avoid recriminations over how the Bloomberg piece had played. But with the Bill Murray circus playing to packed houses all over the world, he had mentioned on Twitter that he would honor the clause. He was playing, of course; it was all part of the immersive landscape that Cilvaringz had promised him for Plan B, where he and us faced off in public, manufactured a beef, and then sent the album skidding out into the world on a stagecraft roller coaster.

But how could the whole situation be harnessed into a new

three-act performance, and how could we build in an option to possibly get the album back for real? Was there a way to lay the groundwork for two possible outcomes on the back of the same strategy? Cilvaringz?

It went like this. Cilvaringz finally managed to get hold of Martin and pitched him a new version of Plan B. We would send a tweet saying this

> Ready to implement heist clause. We had @cilvaringz1 send @martinshkreli amended contract 3 days ago. No reply. #coldfeet

To which Martin would reply

> Saw nothing. Resend.

At which point we would send a legally binding amendment to him, signed by our side. He would sign it, photograph it, send it back, and put it on Twitter for all the world to see that the Bill Murray clause was now just as real as the rest of the sales contract. He would caption the photo of the newly minted amendment with

> Signed. Warning you all. Don't fuck with me.

We would then coordinate a robbery, with Martin's full knowledge, that would involve RZA, GZA, Cilvaringz, Raekwon, Ghostface, and Bill Murray. Martin would be livestreaming, as he so regularly did, and suddenly, live online, six masked figures would burst into the room behind him and drag him off his chair with a "drugged" handkerchief over his mouth. With Martin playing unconscious, Bill Murray would take off his balaclava, peer absently into the webcam, and take a line straight out of *Pulp Fiction:* "Everybody be cool. This is a robbery."

Cue total confusion and scintillating excitement among all who were watching. They would immediately flood onto social networks with the news that Martin Shkreli was being robbed live online by Bill Murray and the Wu-Tang Clan and it would go instantly viral. With the stream still playing, the six members of the heist team would search his office looking for the album, and while doing so, stumble across the blueprints for cancer and AIDS cures that Martin was planning to sell to the highest bidder and Photoshopped pictures under his pillow of him cuddling Taylor Swift. We would find the book that went with the album, the box itself, but not the holy grail of the two CDs. With sirens getting louder and the police swooping on his home, the crack team of infiltrators would make their escape, but without the album.

Bloodied but unbowed, Martin would recover his bravado and lay down an ultimatum. If the world felt this strongly about his keeping the album private and if the Clan was going to these lengths to get it back, he would offer the fans a single opportunity. Thirty-six days to sell thirty-six thousand copies. If the target was reached, he would release the album and accept that it belonged to the world. If it wasn't, he would destroy it live online. Snap the CDs clean in half. It was now or never to own a copy of *Once Upon a Time in Shaolin.*

There were two issues. One was explaining our sudden volteface on the idea of a private album. If the whole idea of a singlecopy album had been ours in the first place, then how did we justify suddenly trying to steal it back simply because the buyer had proved controversial? Simple. He kept insisting that he would never listen to it, and that flew in the face of all the promises he'd made to us pre-Daraprim. A work of art could be treasured by one man alone, but if he didn't treasure it, then he forfeited his rights to it. And the second fly in the ointment was colluding with the Most Hated Man in America in a stunt that could only amplify his notoriety and mainline oxygen into his bid for publicity.

But here was the really ingenious part. Once Martin had signed the amendment, made it legal, and let the Heist Squad into his house, there was nothing to prevent us from stealing the album back for real. He would think we were all in on it together until the handkerchief went over his mouth and it really was drugged. And then it was open season. The clause was watertight; there had been no illegal entry, as he had let us into his house, and by stringing him along and making him feel part of the plan, we would have tricked him into losing the album for real.

So with two possible, parallel outcomes, the next few weeks would dictate which path we chose. Martin was thrilled about the prospect—he just loved anything that involved weaving comic book excess into the real world. But the plan needed to be carefully calibrated and the script needed to be followed at all costs in order for this to work.

HA! We had underestimated the sheer, mind-boggling insanity of Mr. Shkreli.

With the heist plan(s) activated, we needed to get hold of Bill Murray. Famous for being off radar and generally a nightmare to get in touch with, the feelers went out and backroom Hollywood channels were tapped. In a cruel twist of irony, it turned out that Bill Murray had been in Marrakech right up until two days before, attending the Marrakech Film Festival. It was just the latest gust of unfathomably unlikely coincidence to blow across the bow, and it came as a knife to the heart. We had contacts among the festival management, and organizing a sit-down in Marrakech would have been remarkably simple. And yet—even though it felt like a missed opportunity, it did imply that the universe was playing comedy poker with us again. Of all the film festivals in all the world at that exact time . . . you could interpret it as playful encouragement as much as a chance gone begging.

So, Martin . . . Oh, Martin, Martin, Martin . . . Within hours of agreeing to the initial script of the Bill Murray heist plan with him, he gave an interview to Justin Hunte at HipHopDX, the biggest hip-hop site in the world. And to put it mildly, he had lost his fucking mind.

It all started absurdly enough, with Martin claiming he would post the $2 million bail for rapper Bobby Shmurda on charges of conspiracy to commit murder. So far, so quirky. And then he went so far off the fucking reservation that he ended up somewhere near Saturn.

It seemed that Martin had a few dramatic flourishes of his own to add to the brewing beef we were cooking up. Clearly he felt our script was too tame and, convinced that we were all in this together, proceeded to diss RZA in the most extraordinary manner imaginable.

> I bought the most expensive album in the history of mankind and fucking RZA is talking shit behind my back and online in plain sight. I'm just getting pissed off. That's not the way I do business. If I hand you $2 million, fucking show me some respect. At least have the decency to say nothing or "no comment." The guy

says ". . . before his business practices came to light."
What the fuck does that mean? I fucking make money.
That's what I do. That's why I can fucking afford a
fucking $2 million album. What do you think I do,
make cookies? No, motherfucker. I sell drugs.
[Laughs] I felt insulted.

And then it got worse. Way fucking worse.

I met the guy at the Soho House. The place doesn't
impress me. The guy sits down. We talk for a half an
hour. We didn't really get to know each other in any
way, shape, or form. That's why I said that we didn't
have much in common because we talked for maybe
an hour. I've had meetings where I was supposed to be
talking to someone for an hour and we end up talking
for six hours because we're so interested in what we
have to say. We've all been there. That's not what
happened. Motherfucker came in. He was late. We sat
down for maybe forty-five minutes at most. He left and
was like, "Man, this is the man that needs to buy this
album." I've been behind a lot of deals. I know when
I'm being bullshitted. You don't have to fucking fake it.
But I still wanted the album. We definitely didn't have
much in common. The guy is fucking full of himself,
talking about how his shit is the best ever, how fucking
Bobby Digital was the best shit ever. I wasn't feeling
him at all. I figured it was another arrogant rapper.
How many of them do you need to meet? . . . I'd
encourage him to shut the fuck up before he goes a

little too far. We'll see what happens. I think he's a
smart man. He definitely acts like his shit doesn't stink
and he invented rap. This concept of selling one
album, this shit's backfiring for him now . . ."

And he finished off tastefully with

If Taylor Swift wants to come over and suck my dick,
I'll play it for her.

Jesus fucking Christ, what was WRONG with this dude?
Apart from the fact that he'd told Bloomberg less than a week
before that he'd really liked RZA when he met him, he didn't
seem to grasp the gravity of what he was saying. RZA is one of
the least arrogant people out there—he's never been one for show
or bragging, and this made him look like a total prick. And
worse, no one has ever dissed RZA or the Clan like that. Ever.
There had to be retaliation for this, whether through words, fists,
or maybe even bullets from a Staten Island crew who wouldn't
let the Clan get dissed by this fuck.

This was spiraling out of control, and the first casualty was
the Bill Murray heist plan. After the shit Martin had said, there
was no way we could come back with some vaguely challenging tweets about a fucking clause. This had just escalated into a
whole new, very unpleasant, and very dangerous realm.

RZA was surprised, to say the least. We tried to tell him that
Martin thought he was playing a character, but his family had
seen quotes from the interview. This had gone very dark, and
whether Martin was for real—which seemed impossible, as RZA
had always been correct and polite with him—or whether he was

tripping on his own unhinged version of the "play," he was clearly as dangerous a liability in the scheming business as he was in the pharmaceutical business.

As RZA tried to call him for the first time since the closing to hear from Martin's own mouth what the fuck he thought he was up to, Martin upped the ante even further, taking out the inner CD case of the album on a livestream and using it as a fucking coaster. I mean, he was certainly doing a bang-up job of making the fans hate him more than ever and creating the environment for a folkloric caper, but he seemed not to have taken into consideration how far he was painting us into a corner where we had to come heavy on him. The whole scenario looked like it would inevitably move from comedy action into something bloodcurdlingly sinister, whether any of us liked it or not. Wu-Tang Clan Ain't Nuthing ta Fuck Wit. And there's an awful lot of gangsta motherfuckers who'd be delighted to step to Martin first—no matter what anyone said. Man's going down.

RZA was awaiting a callback from Martin to explain himself. Cilvaringz was in the planning bunker seeing if anything could be even remotely salvaged from the burning wreckage of Martin's HipHopDX interview. And I was at my lowest ebb. Thanks to Martin, we'd just lost control of the whole narrative and shit was looking like it might get way too fucking real.

And then . . . out of a clear blue sky, the FBI arrested Martin in a dawn raid.

It was December 17. $1+7=8$.

FEDERAL

The *New York Times* reported:

> At 6 a.m. Thursday, F.B.I. agents arrested Mr. Shkreli,
> 32, at his Murray Hill apartment. He was arraigned in
> Federal District Court in Brooklyn on securities fraud
> and wire fraud charges.

The article continued,

> Mr. Shkreli could have been a quintessential archetype
> for the immigrant's dream of American success. He
> grew up in a crowded apartment on Ocean Avenue
> in Brooklyn, the son of Albanian immigrants who
> worked janitorial and other side jobs to support him
> and his three siblings.

This was perhaps the most poignant aspect of Martin's arc. It
was the self-made immigrant backstory that had impressed RZA
at Soho House all those months ago. He hadn't been born with

a silver spoon up his ass, he had grafted and cut corners and hustled and dragged his way to the top with nothing but his wits and his determination. Except somewhere along the way, a circuit had burned that kept pushing him over the edge of reason. He didn't need to become the most notorious villain in America. He didn't need to revel in the rivers of hatred directed at him. He didn't need to keep kicking every hornet's nest he found. And he didn't need to systematically go too far on every single front.

Whether the charges were true or not wasn't something we could judge, though you would imagine that the FBI and federal prosecutors wouldn't commit to such a high-profile arrest if they didn't have a solid case. Surely their Director of Communications had pulled them up and said, "Guys, you better be sure or we're going to look like bitches." But Martin had flown way too close to the sun. You almost wanted to send him an illustrated copy of the Daedalus and Icarus story. He had pissed the entire country off.

The whole of corporate America needed him gone. He was attracting way too much attention to the mercenary practices entrenched throughout the system, all propped up by lobbyist donations and political corruption. I say corruption, but it's all legal, because that's how institutional corruption works—the guys taking the money make the laws. The pharmaceutical industry in particular needed to discredit him as a crook so as to distance their business practices from his. Politicians didn't really want the price gouging fight—if they did, American healthcare wouldn't be the disgraceful morass of inequity that it is, and neither Democrat candidate really wanted to ensure every Pharma firm contributed vast sums to their Republican opponents by proposing concrete measures to rein them in. As for the Republicans, Martin Shkreli was probably the only immigrant in America they approved of, as their equation of wealth with moral worth must make him a fucking saint. But even Trump wasn't dumb enough to wave that flag publicly.

The public hated him, of course, so the overwhelming reaction from boardrooms and protesters alike was "Karma." There seemed to be universal delight at his downfall, which we found a little distasteful. That's the thing: it's so easy to hate a guy you've never met, a lot trickier when he's actually been pretty cool with you. Reconciling personal instincts with outrage at the things someone has done is always an engrossing moral dilemma. I'm sure Stalin was a fucking charmer over brandy.

But what about the album? By 8 a.m. Eastern Time, speculation was rife about its fate. Social media was crackling with rumors about the album having been seized by the feds. My instinctive reaction was "Oh fuck no," until the kneejerk stabilized and a whole different perspective dawned.

Wait a minute. I had visions of the final scene in *Raiders of the Lost Ark,* where the ark is filed away into the anonymity of a government warehouse. Jesus, if this album wasn't mythological enough already, disappearing into federal custody would certainly up the game. And then, after a few months in a government stronghold, it might well get auctioned off in an asset forfeiture sale. The idea of the album being auctioned all over again, this time by the fucking FBI, was just too seductive. We could buy it back and release it. Or just watch as fans started the bidding at a dollar. It was gold. Pure fucking gold. The FBI auctioning the album. This is such stuff as dreams are made on.

Reality check, though. It was highly unlikely the FBI would seize the album unless they had proof it had been bought with illegally obtained funds. But then again, they might freeze his assets. And if he was convicted of fraud, then someone would be seizing the album, whether it was the FBI or creditors in the various lawsuits filed against him. It wasn't an unrealistic scenario, but it was one that might not be feasible before a conviction. Shares in his new company, KaloBios, had plummeted 50 percent in thirteen minutes before trading was suspended, and the fact that the feds had arrested his lawyer as a co-conspirator to break privilege and narrow his escape routes was all too telling. They meant business.

And then a tweet so surreal that it may even have surpassed the Bill Murray heist clause was posted by the FBI:

> #Breaking no seizure warrant at the arrest of Martin Shkreli
> today, which means we didn't seize the Wu-Tang Clan album

It was so far-fetched that you kept having to pinch yourself. It was right up there with the CIA's tweet from 2014 saying "No we don't know where Tupac is." Except this was real and not a government agency trying to show its human side. Even Eric B and Rakim had replied to the FBI with the immortal words "Don't Sweat the Technique."

And at the prosecutor's press conference, the album was clearly the subject of as much interest as the charges themselves. When confronted with a barrage of questions concerning the fate of the album, United States Attorney Robert L. Capers replied, "I wondered how long it was going to take to get to that. We're not aware of where he got the funds that he raised to buy the Wu-Tang Clan album."

The federal prosecutor's name was Capers. You just couldn't

invent this shit. All he needed to do now was peel off his mask and reveal himself as Bill Murray.

Martin had been accused of running a Ponzi scheme across his businesses. Financial cases are notoriously slow moving, so one had to assume that the investigation had started when Martin left his previous company, Retrophin, in a storm of fraud allegations. Consequently, it must have predated the Daraprim price hike and his ascent to the Scepter of Evil. Whether the arrest had been accelerated to shut him up was an open question, but the situation looked pretty bleak for him, and no matter what happened, it would probably be a year or so before the case went to trial, and the trial would be lengthy.

We all waited to see where the chips fell, and two days after the arrest, Martin called Cilvaringz. His voice sounded totally different, far more subdued and pensive about the realities of his situation. No one from our side had spoken to him since that car crash HipHopDX interview, and Martin had no idea that he had pushed things to the brink. As far as he was concerned, he was playing a role, and the more outlandish the results were, the more effectively he had done his part. Cilvaringz was almost speechless, trying to get Martin to see the impact of his behavior. And apparently, if the FBI hadn't intervened, he had been planning to take things even further. In an extraordinary twist, it turned out that he had gotten hold of some replica AK-47s and was about to post a video with him and his posse surrounding the album holding the guns and calling out the Clan with lines like "A message to ODB. Make some room in heaven, because your brothers are about to join you."

WHAT THE FUCK WAS WRONG WITH THIS GUY?

Using a dead Clan member to threaten the murder of the rest of the Clan? What the fuck would constitute "too far" in his book? That would have been tantamount to inciting a gang war. And the most incredible thing of all was that he had apparently told the feds all about it, no doubt to explain the presence of replica AK-47s in his house. It was insanity on a different level from anything we had imagined possible, and Martin just couldn't see it. He was like a kid playing with fire—it was all a bit of fun, with an inexplicable inability to foresee the consequences. And that basically summed up Martin in a nutshell.

Meanwhile, the Internet was a rampant inferno. It was like Christmas in an open-source gossip column. The press struggled to keep up with the shards of imagination people kept hurling toward what was rapidly becoming one of the year's strangest stories. There was talk of the album being cursed, which was a supremely intoxicating idea, taking us straight back to the sands of Egypt and the excavation of this buried treasure. When RZA had called the album the scepter of an Egyptian king all those many months ago, little did we know that the story would come full circle with a curse legend. The story of Martin's arrest was summarized beautifully by a meme that quite simply read, "100% of people who bought the Wu-Tang Clan album have been arrested." Classic.

With the federal government circling the album, one enterprising dude named Andrew Wiseman filed a Freedom of Information Act request for the album, promising to give copies of it away in return for a charitable donation if he ever actually had the music handed over to him by the Department of Justice. Others seemed convinced that we had ratted Shkreli out, either as simple revenge or as a distraction ploy to allow the album to be stolen back, and the Bill Murray dream scenario simply had too much mileage in it for the world to leave it alone. Shortly before Christmas, the rapper ProbCause teamed up with director Elijah Alvarado to create a short animated video of what the heist might look like. With vocal samples lifted from *Coffee and Cigarettes,* the "Wu-Tang Financial" sketch on Dave Chappelle, Martin saying he wished he'd raised the price higher, and other assorted gems, it was beginning to look like the ultimate success.

That's the thing about success. If you strip ego and control out of it, then surely it's defined by how many people feel inspired to contribute, whether it be their attention or a new thread to the creative tapestry. An album that had started out to redefine ideas about listening to recorded music had become the world's most untouchable, exclusive, and alienating piece of music, before morphing into a unifying force on the Internet that triggered jokes, skits, and plays from all four corners of the globe. And STILL no one had listened to it. This story had been one of paradox and irony, and as the tide rushed in, the box continued to guard its secrets while the world made merry on its tale. I'd call that a success—just a very unusual one.

But would there be one final twist? As Martin's finances tightened in the wake of his arrest and the chaos his companies were thrown into deepened, he contacted us to see if there might be a way for him to recoup his investment. Resale would be out of the question, as very few people would be queuing up to give him their money, even before the trust issue implicit in the deal. Who would trust Martin Shkreli not to have held on to a copy?

He wondered if there might be another narrative along the lines of the Bill Murray heist that could allow him to make his money back, and made it very clear that he was open to ideas.

It was a tricky one. He had proved totally unreliable in any kind of scripted scheme, and I advised against any action before it blew up in our faces. And while the Bill Murray heist idea was built around the possibility of recovering the album for real, it was difficult to envision a new scenario that held any honor for us. And then RZA stepped in with a sentence that changed the game: "A heist can take many forms."

Cilvaringz immediately set himself to deconstructing that cryptic statement, and within a couple of days, he had a fresh plot on the stove. We could resurrect Plan B. If we brought back our fake buyer, he could take the album off Martin's hands and play out the plan as originally intended. Martin wouldn't receive any money up front, but would recover his investment out of the limited-edition sale. The only real issue was that no one trusted Martin not to suddenly turn up at a press conference with his replica AK-47s, inject his own deranged flourish into proceedings, and scupper a tight, complex narrative.

Reflecting on what RZA had said, Cilvaringz mapped out a blueprint. To ensure Martin didn't go off the reservation again, our involvement would be conditional on his uploading the album to escrow and signing a watertight contract that transferred all rights back to us if he strayed from the agreed protocols. None of us by this stage believed Martin would be able to restrain himself from doing something crazy, and by instituting this clause, we would give him enough rope to hang himself. It was yet another game of chess, using our opponent's instincts against him and potentially seeing the album legally returned to us. At which point we could put it straight out to the public.

If he managed to somehow keep himself together, the public got the album, he got his money back, and we would have the chance to play out a whole new phase with Plan B.

If he couldn't control himself, we would have heisted the album by heisting his mind, employing his own psychology to legally return the album to us. It was a fucking genius plan.

Alas, that condition proved too harsh for him, and he decided to find his own way with the album. Such a shame. A fourth act gone begging.

UNFINISHED SYMPHONY

Take a kid with a dream. A legendary hip-hop group. A cultural crisis that saw social and technological changes reshape the economics and the experience of music. Six years of secret recordings. A casing worthy of a king. A single artifact. Hallowed establishment institutions. An iconoclastic auction house. The world's foremost museum of modern art. A bidding war. Endless crises of conscience. An angry mob. A furious beef. A sale. A villain of Lex Luthor–like proportions. Bill Murray. The FBI. The Internet gone fucking wild.

It had all started with a question, and ended with another. Through the slings and arrows of outrageous fortune, the perpetual soul-searching, the highs, the lows, the contradictions, and the clarity, this album had transcended music to become a cultural icon. What that icon represented varied wildly depending on who you asked—was it the best of modern society, was it the worst of modern society, or was it like any real work of art, morally neutral and existing far beyond the control of its creators? It had begun as a protest in the name of music, and yet here we were with hardly a note having been played. It had begun as a clarion cry for the people and had ended as a joker on capitalism's card table. It began as high art and ended as popular art, inclusive art, open-source art, where creative minds contributed to the unfolding tale no matter their status, their background, or their connections.

Martin Shkreli, the man who turned this whole voyage on its head, had been a blessing in so many ways. He brought a whole new dimension of drama, of cautionary hubris, of dystopian possibility, and of unimaginable lunacy. It wasn't anywhere near the outcome we had hoped for, but in retrospect, his buying the album did more for the debate and the entertainment than anyone else on earth. As we spoke to him more frequently after his arrest, he seemed like a tragic figure. He had trolled the world with a horrifying vision of the future, and he had actually made our point better than we could have done ourselves. And even what that point was had been through a thousand revolutions.

When Martin told the *Wall Street Journal* that his behavior had been a "social experiment," the press used that as another weapon against him, but to us, it was vividly apparent how true that statement was. He had never been anything other than cool, honest, direct, and correct with us—and even the batshit crazy aspects like his rant against RZA had been part of what he saw as his theater. There was no doubt in our mind that he was nuts, but not in that smirking, evil way. No, he was intelligent, lonely, bored, contrarian, and the star of a movie in his own mind. We had to doubt whether he could even hold a Ponzi scheme together, as his penchant for getting overexcited and committing some insanely inappropriate act seemed to defy the presentation of him as a calculating criminal. Alas, he had misjudged his public, and by the time he tried to tell the world that it had all been a joke, he had already cried wolf far too many times. Whether the Daraprim hike fell into the category of provocation or copycat capitalism in an unregulated culture of greed is something time will tell, but Martin is the kind of figure the Greeks would have had a field day with. Tragedy and comedy in the selfsame play.

I said early on that we had hoisted a sail and launched the album to chart its own fate. And so it had. We had guided the rudder where we could, sailed tropical lagoons, and furiously bailed water out of a sinking ship. And as we look back and reflect on what was achieved—the world's most expensive album, the debate, the recriminations, the fun, the philosophical introspection, and the full-throated abuse—the most precious achievement of all, at least for me, was that the journey wasn't over.

As I write this, the album's fate remains uncertain. Will Martin be able to hold on to it? Will he suddenly think, Fuck it, and put it out to the public in order to prove he's not America's most evil man? Will Dick Cheney suddenly buy it and give us a far more convincing supervillain? Will the FBI seize it and bury it in a storage warehouse? Will they auction it off in a spectacular art world subversion surrounded by barbed wire? Will they have Alexander Gilkes auction it for them? Will it be hacked, will it leak, will the story live on in new chapters or die a death with Bill Murray reading the last rites? Will someone discover the album in a hundred years at the back of a dusty shelf and release the music to the world? Will it hold its secrets or spill them within weeks? Will it remain Schrödinger's album?

If we had closure, it would be enticingly symmetrical, but ultimately hollow. This artwork is now alive, infused with the energy of millions, and adrift on the white waters of destiny. Anything might happen, and as *Once Upon a Time in Shaolin* dips over the horizon, a new ocean opens up before it. Only the heavens know what the years might bring. I haven't got a fucking clue. And that's the best part.

ACKNOWLEDGMENTS

With huge thanks, love and respect to

Sima and Kew Bozorgmehr
Madeline Williams
Spiral Tribe
Arcadia Spectacular
Wayne Anthony
Nadia Bramante
Dan Cole
Clare Azzougarh
Krissie Ducker
Jane Finigan
Lucinda Prain
David Forrer
Jasmine Faustino
Colin Dickerman
Jimmy and Kate Boyle
Nick Wilde

Zara Williams Bozorgmehr

To Tarik, RZA, and everyone we met along the ride—I hope this book does the adventure we lived some justice.

ABOUT THE AUTHOR

Cyrus Bozorgmehr was the senior advisor on the *Once Upon a Time in Shaolin* project and worked alongside Wu-Tang Clan's RZA and producer Cilvaringz. He lives in Marrakech, Morocco.